TEMPLE GRANDIN

TEMPLE GRANDIN

HOW THE GIRL WHO LOVED COWS EMBRACED AUTISM AND CHANGED THE WORLD

by Sy Montgomery

Houghton Mifflin Harcourt
Boston   New York

For information about permission to reproduce selections from this book, write to
trade.permissions@hmhco.com or to Permissions, Houghton Mifflin Harcourt
Publishing Company, 3 Park Avenue, 19th Floor, New York, New York 10016.

www.hmhco.com

The text of this book is set in Minion and Pencil Pete.
Line illustrations are taken from the Dover Pictorial Archive.
Photo copyright and credits for design drawings appear on page 142.

Library of Congress Cataloging-in-Publication Data is on file.

ISBN: 978-0-547-44315-7 hardcover
ISBN: 978-0-544-33909-5 paperback

Manufactured in China
SCP 10 9 8 7
4500666352

In Memory of Oliver Carey

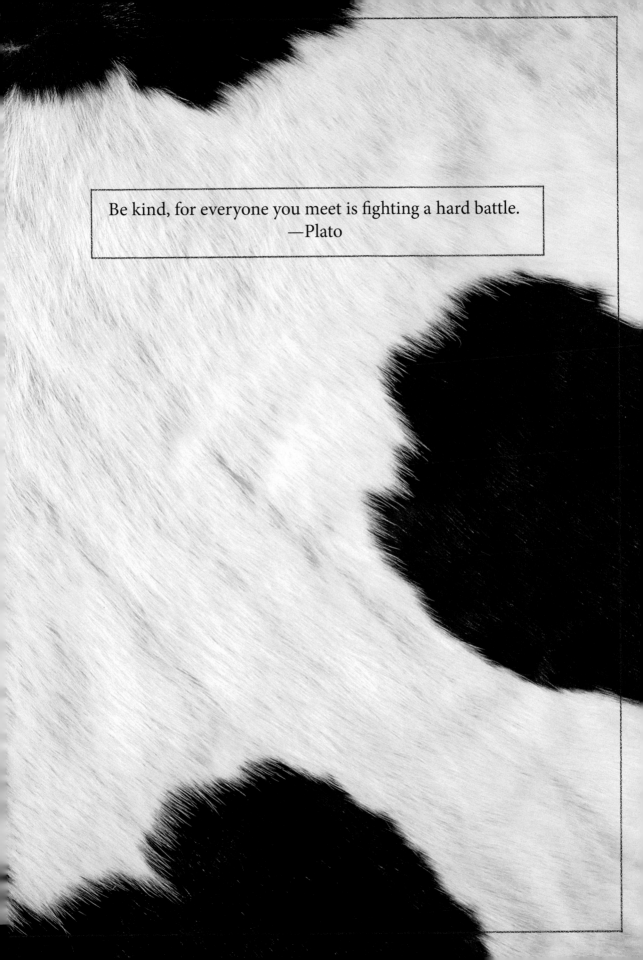

Be kind, for everyone you meet is fighting a hard battle.
—Plato

FOREWORD
BY TEMPLE GRANDIN

Throughout my career, I have worked to improve the treatment of farm animals because we owe it to domestic animals to give them a decent life. My work with animals started in high school, when I spent time in a stable taking care of nine horses. At that time, my world revolved around grooming, riding, and showing horses in local shows. Summer trips to my aunt's ranch introduced me to the West and to cattle. As I became more and more interested in cattle, I had increasing concerns about how they were being handled and treated. In the early 1970s, when I started working with livestock, many of the cowboys were really rough with the animals. This motivated me to find better ways of handling cows when they were run through a chute for vaccinations.

Today, half of the cattle in the United States and Canada are handled in systems I have designed for meat-packing plants. Some of my greatest reforms came about through working with McDonald's and other major restaurant chains on animal-welfare audits and meat-plant inspections. Audits and inspections by these large meat buyers forced plant managers to correctly operate the systems I had designed. To ensure that animals are treated calmly and with respect requires both well-designed equipment and managers committed to good practices.

Before I started my career with animals, I was one of those kids who did not fit in with the rest of the crowd. There are many kids like me, with various labels such as autism, Asperger's syndrome, ADHD, dyslexia, or other learning disabilities. What saved me and enabled me to succeed were my love of making things and creating art. In elementary school, my teachers and my mother always encouraged my interest in art. When I grew up, I chose a career designing livestock facilities which allowed me to use my abilities as a visual thinker. Individuals who have been labeled with disabilities — or even just quirky or nerdy kids — often have uneven skills. The ones who become successful in life are those who figure out how to use their unique abilities and passions in work they can pursue with other people.

One advantage to growing up in the 1950s was that there were lots of hands-on activities that all of us participated in. In elementary school, I loved anything that could fly, like kites and toy airplanes. I invented a kite shaped like a bird, made from heavy art paper, to fly behind my bike. I experimented with the shape of the wings so it would fly at a steeper angle, and I bent the tips up to increase the lift. Today, when I fly on a jet, I get real satisfaction when I look at the plane's upturned wingtips. The ratio of the area of the upturned winglet to the area of the jet's wing is approximately the same as it was on my bird kites. That was the beginning of my life of inventing and building things. My favorite book when I was a child was about famous inventors.

When I was younger, I learned both design skills and patience from experimenting with paper kites or developing an improved parachute made from old scarves. I spent hours experimenting and then testing my designs. To prevent the strings on my parachute from tangling, I attached them to crossbars made from bent coat hangers and tape. I tried many different designs — I learned that it takes a lot of patience and time to figure out the best solutions.

I also had to learn to use my abilities to do work that was useful to other people. During my teen years I built a gate that a driver could open from inside the car — that was shown in the HBO movie about me. Along with caring for horses, I did lots of carpentry work and learned many useful work skills.

Some of my childhood friends were interviewed for this book. My friends and I enjoyed activities in which we had a shared interest, such as art, horseback riding, or electronics. I suggest that all of you get involved with activities that you can do with other students, such as Boy Scouts or Girl Scouts, art projects, school plays, band, robotics, computer club, or the school newspaper or webpage. These hands-on activities saved me from the total torture of being bullied and teased. By finding friends who like the same activities that you like, you can avoid the bullies. And these projects taught me practical problem solving and helped prepare me for a professional career. I hope that my story will encourage you to find your own passions and to follow them.

Even as a baby, Temple seemed different.

CHAPTER ONE
SENSES ON FIRE

Every day at school, she dreaded the sound: the loud, deep ring of the school bell. The janitor rang it at the end of each class: *CLANG! CLANG! CLANG!* Most kids were happy to hear it — but for Temple Grandin, the ringing of the bell hurt like a dentist's drill hitting a nerve. She covered her ears, but she could still hear it. There was no escape.

For Temple, ordinary sensations could be torture. The grip of a stretchy wool hat pulled over her ears made her head feel like it was caught in a vise. New socks and underwear scratched like sandpaper. Wearing a stiff petticoat beneath her church dress on Sunday felt like needles stabbing her skin. Sometimes it felt as if her senses were on fire.

If a teacher wore strong perfume, Temple couldn't even think. The odor drowned out the meaning of the writing on the blackboard, overwhelmed the sound of the teacher's voice. Human voices themselves made little sense when Temple was small: although some noises were painfully loud, words were terribly unclear. If somebody said, "Joe walked to school" she heard only, "oh ah ool." The adults around her sounded as if they were speaking gibberish. Sometimes the only way she could communicate was to throw a temper tantrum. She would howl her frustration wordlessly, break things, flap her hands, and cry.

Nobody — least of all Temple herself — understood what was wrong.

Almost from the start, Temple's mother knew that her first child was different. Most babies love to be cuddled, but Temple would stiffen and pull away from her mother's arms. Most children look with special interest into people's faces, particularly the eyes. Temple wouldn't meet another's gaze. And while most toddlers begin to talk around age two, Temple didn't speak at all.

Temple's mother loved her. But Temple was a difficult child to love. She did so few of the things that typical children do to make people love them.

She didn't laugh. She didn't smile when tickled. She didn't hug her mother or father or hold out her arms to be picked up. At age two and three and even four, she never said, "I love you, Mommy."

Rather than play, Temple drew on the walls with pencils and crayons. She peed on the floor. Instead of playing with cardboard puzzles, she chewed them up and spat them out. Temple didn't speak until she was five — and even then, her words came out in spasms, not sentences. She might blurt out a word like "ice" or "mine" or "no," but only when she was upset. Most of the time, nobody understood what Temple was saying. No one understood what she was feeling. And nobody could guess what — and some wondered even *if*—she was thinking. Her own father thought Temple was retarded. He wanted to send her away to live in a mental hospital.

Temple is now in her sixties, but she still remembers the frustrations she felt as a child. She recalls one day in kindergarten when the teacher was showing the class how to sort words according to their first letter.

In a workbook with pictures, the teacher asked the students to mark the objects whose names began with a B. The book had pictures of a suitcase, a birdbath, a chair...By that time, Temple knew the alphabet, and she went right to work. She recognized the pictures immediately and began to sort them in her mind. The suitcase was what her parents packed when they traveled — a bag, or baggage — so Temple marked that picture with a B. The birdbath was shown in a flowery garden, so that surely belonged with the Gs. Temple was pleased with her answers.

But the teacher marked almost all of Temple's answers wrong. Temple couldn't explain what she'd been thinking. She knew she was right. The word "baggage" really started with the letter B, and "garden" really did begin with G! Temple had a good mind. In fact, she was quite brilliant, though no one realized it then. Her mind didn't work the way most people's minds do.

When she was three, Temple was diagnosed with autism (*AW-tizm*), a disorder of the brain that is still poorly understood. Autism affects people in different ways. For some people with autism, words never make sense. Some never learn to speak, never make friends, never come to understand the world as anything but one painful, random event after another. Others, whose autism is milder, may be nerdy, geeky kids who grow up to make computers in Silicon Valley. Many are very bright, but their skills are uneven.

Like most children with autism, Temple felt assaulted by her own sensory system. Her ears and eyes and nose worked fine, but the information carried to her brain was distorted. Sounds were too loud, scents too strong, words garbled. Sometimes a bright light or a whirring fan was

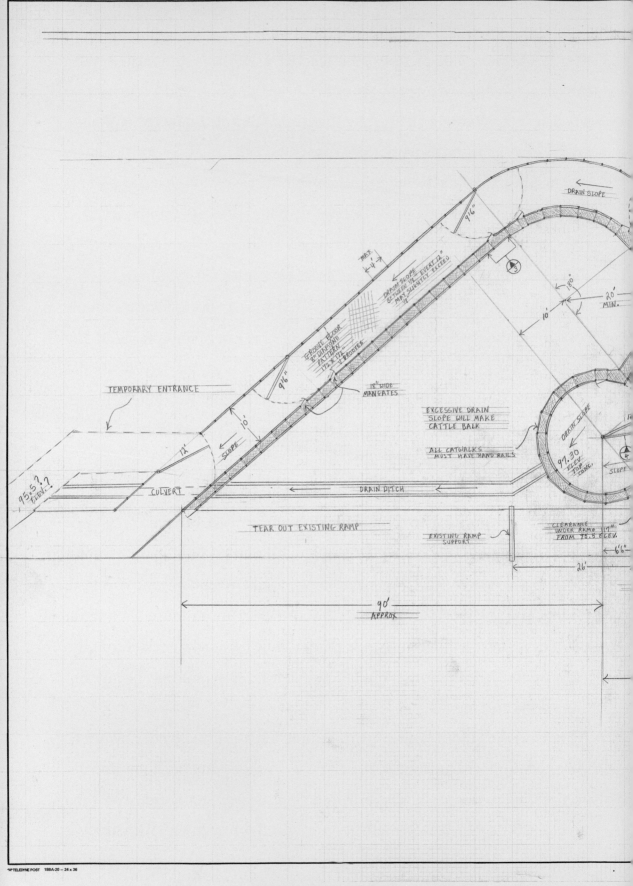

Thinking in pictures helps Temple design facilities like this one, with features that protect cattle from fear.

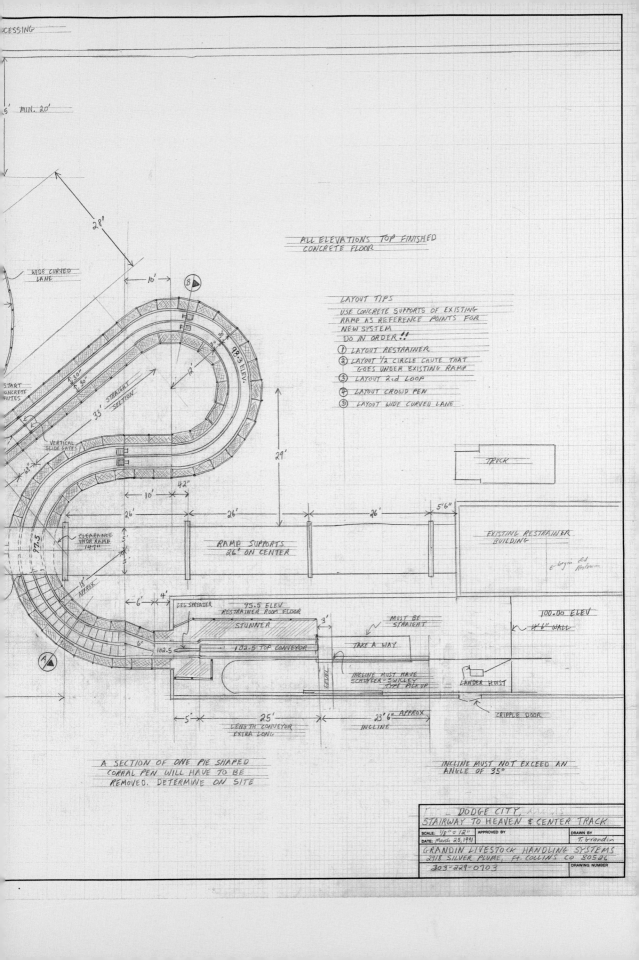

CESSING

5' MIN. 20'

28'

WIDE CURVED LANE

10'

8

ALL ELEVATIONS TOP FINISHED
CONCRETE FLOOR

LAYOUT TIPS
USE CONCRETE SUPPORTS OF EXISTING
RAMP AS REFERENCE POINTS FOR
NEW SYSTEM
DO IN ORDER!!
① LAYOUT RESTRAINER
② LAYOUT ½ CIRCLE CHUTE THAT
   GOES UNDER EXISTING RAMP
③ LAYOUT 2nd LOOP
④ LAYOUT CROWD PEN
⑤ LAYOUT WIDE CURVED LANE

98.3 ELEV.

30"
30"

STRAIGHT SECTION

33'

START CONCRETE CHUTES

130"
30"

VERTICAL SLIDE GATES

63"

42"

10'

29'

TRUCK

26'

26'

26'

5'6"

EXISTING RESTRAINER
BUILDING

97.5

CLEARANCE UNDER RAMP
147"

5'

RAMP SUPPORTS
26' ON CENTER

E begin ed
Restrainer

100.00 ELEV

18 APPROX

6'   4'

LEG SPREADER   95.5 ELEV
RESTRAINER ROOM FLOOR

3'

MUST BE
STRAIGHT

4'6" WALL

A

STUNNER

102.5   102.5 TOP CONVEYOR

6'

TAKE A WAY

INCLINE MUST HAVE
SCHUYLER - SWICLEY
TYPE PICK UP

LANDER HOIST

LEVEL

CRIPPLE DOOR

5'

25'
LENGTH CONVEYOR
EXTRA LONG

23' 6" APPROX
INCLINE

A SECTION OF ONE PIE SHAPED
CORRAL PEN WILL HAVE TO BE
REMOVED. DETERMINE ON SITE

INCLINE MUST NOT EXCEED AN
ANGLE OF 35°

DODGE CITY, KANSAS		
STAIRWAY TO HEAVEN & CENTER TRACK		
SCALE: 1/8"=12" APPROVED BY		DRAWN BY
DATE: March 25, 1991		T. Grandin
GRANDIN LIVESTOCK HANDLING SYSTEMS		
2918 SILVER PLUME, Ft. COLLINS CO 80526		
303-229-0703		DRAWING NUMBER

physically painful. She loved flapping flags, but the sight of one was so engrossing, she found it difficult to concentrate on anything else.

To escape the painful noises, confusing words, and overwhelming sensations, Temple would twirl. Many kids like to twirl in circles, but Temple would twirl for hours on end. She would also spin coins and jar lids and watch them for hours. By retreating into her own world, she could screen out the confusion around her.

In a sandbox or at the beach, Temple loved to dribble sand through her fingers. She would watch the way the sand dropped through her hands, absorbed completely in the beauty of each grain. She noticed and remembered every detail: the sizes, colors, shapes, the way the light made some grains into beautiful, gleaming gems, and others into glinting shards of gold or silver.

Temple saw almost everything in exceptionally rich detail. She could recall every image almost as if it were a photograph or a movie. When she thought, her mind would run a videotape of images. Each image was specific — not a generic representation or an idea, but the *exact* image of a thing or event that she had once seen. When she thought, there were no words. Words were difficult and strange. Temple thought entirely in pictures. She still does to this day.

Most of us think mainly in words or ideas. The pictures in our minds tend to be fuzzy. Quick: What color are your best friend's eyes? How many windows are on the front of your school? Do you have freckles on your face? Without looking, can you remember how many? Where are they?

When you hear the words "church steeple," you probably see in your mind a sort of general, tall white pointy structure on the roof of a house of worship. But when Temple thinks "church steeple," she sees a series of specific pictures: the steeple on St. Paul's Episcopal Church in Dedham, Massachusetts, where she grew up; the one with a giant cross in Fort Collins, Colorado, where she now lives and teaches at the university;

Temple, as a young woman, gazes at one of her early designs made real at an Arizona beef facility.

an odd, round steeple at another church in the same town; a square one made of cinderblocks painted white, with green trim on the slanted louvers, where the church bell hangs. (Temple calls that church "Our Lady of the Louvers.") On and on the pictures go, like a computer search of images projected rapidly inside her head: a succession of real, individual church steeples, in complete and accurate detail.

As a child, and even after she became an adult, Temple didn't realize that most people don't think this way. But her ability to think in pic-

Temple today.

tures, along with the unusual way her autistic brain handled sounds, sights, and feelings, would turn Temple Grandin into an international hero to both people and animals.

Temple, her family, and teachers worked hard to overcome her problems with words. She learned to speak so well that she now travels around the world and lectures in front of thousands of people. She has written more than four hundred articles and ten books. She has outgrown some of the pain of loud high-pitched noises, scratchy fabrics, and distracting lights, and she has learned how to cope with the discomforts that remain. And thanks to lots of hard work, the baby who wouldn't let her own mother hug her has grown up to be warm and friendly in her own way.

But Temple's story is about far more than overcoming a disability. Temple's life shows us the courage and creativity of a person who found the blessings of autism — the blessings of a different kind of brain that, along with its challenges, may also bring extraordinary gifts.

The feeling is mutual: cattle feel calm around Temple, and she feels calm around them.

9855

Temple Grandin, sixty-three, sits at the big mahogany table in the university's paneled conference room. She has ducked in here between classes to make a phone call to a client. From the walls of the room, portraits of past department heads of Colorado State University — distinguished older men in business suits and cowboy hats — seem to be looking on from their picture frames. If they could hear her, they'd be in on an unusual conversation.

"It's just *hideously disgusting*," Temple says forcefully into her cell phone. She's talking to a top manager of a multimillion-dollar restaurant chain. Wearing a denim shirt, a striped vest, black western necktie, and black jeans with a silver belt buckle shaped like the head of a steer, Temple is five foot eight and weighs 170 pounds. She is strong, tall, and confident. You would never guess she was shy — much less autistic.

"I've had another company call me about buying this kind of meat. It's called bob veal," she tells the executive on the phone. "These are infant calves too young to even walk, usually Holsteins. Infant calves are thrown off cattle trucks because the poor things can't even walk down the ramp to the slaughterhouse. There is no humane way to process that kind of animal."

After talking with Temple, the company decides it won't buy any bob veal and won't serve it to its millions of customers.

"That veal is too gross to eat anyway," Temple says later. She used to have to eat it for lunch in school. It was usually breaded and fried, and so flat it looked as if it had been run over by the school bus. "We used to call it 'elephant scabs'!" she says, and giggles. (The only food that's grosser, in her opinion? Slimy, slippery raw oysters. She calls them "whale boogers.")

Dozens of huge corporations — from restaurant chains like McDonald's and Wendy's to giant meat-packing plants where food animals are slaughtered — consult with Temple about the animals who provide most of North America's meat, eggs, and milk. Her clients don't want to be part of the cruelty that, as humane organizations have shown, is too often standard practice on "factory farms" — huge outdoor facilities or warehouses where the animals are treated like machines instead of thinking, feeling creatures.

These clients come to Temple because she is one of a tiny handful of experts who design pens, walkways, devices, and entire buildings specifically to make the food animals in these big operations calmer and more comfortable. She invents new ways to make sure that livestock handlers are not being cruel to the animals. Half the beef cattle in the United States and Canada, and a growing number overseas, are handled in facilities she has designed. She is working hard to create better conditions for farmed chickens, pigs, and turkeys, too.

For her pioneering work, *Time* magazine named Temple one of its 100 Most Influential People of 2010. (She was number 31 on the list.) *Time* called her "one of the world's most respected advocates for the humane treatment of livestock." The science magazine *Discover* writes, "Temple

Grandin has probably done more to improve welfare for animals at the point of slaughter than any human alive."

Humane activists and the meat industry may argue over many issues, but on one point they agree: Temple Grandin is a godsend for animals. She is the only person in the world who has been honored by People for

Temple lectures around the world on animal behavior and autism.

the Ethical Treatment of Animals as a visionary *and* has been inducted into the Meat Industry Hall of Fame.

After the phone call, Temple heads to the university's equine science class to give a lecture about the minds of animals. She turns on the projector for her PowerPoint presentation, adjusts the focus, and takes her place in front of seventy eager students. "The first thing we're going to talk about," she announces, "is, do horses and other animals actually have emotions? Let's look at the hard science."

She clicks the remote to show dozens of scientific references on the screen. "The research that shows that animals actually have emotions has been summarized by scientists who study the brain," she says. "The fact that animals have emotions is well documented. Their nervous systems are about the same as ours. They have all the same chemicals in the brain. That's why your vet can prescribe the same antianxiety drug for your dog as he does for you! But not all the scientists know this. That's because the different scientific specialties often don't read each other's scientific journals —"

Her cell phone rings. "Excuse me," she says to the students and turns aside. Normally she'd turn her cell phone off during a lecture, but she's expecting some urgent calls. She answers the phone right in front of the class.

"Hello, this is Temple Grandin…"

Already on this December morning, she's taken several calls from the television network HBO about her biopic, starring Claire Danes as Temple, which will be coming out in just a few weeks. The publicists are checking their press release; Temple suggests several changes. She loves the movie, saying the producers did "a brilliant job showing my anxiety, visual thinking, and sensory oversensitivity," but she wants to make sure people know that for dramatic effect the scriptwriters put some events into the film that didn't really happen, changed some of the characters, and altered the timeline. (All her construction projects were recreated for the movie with perfect accuracy.)

This time, though, it's CNN calling. The Humane Society of the United States sent an undercover videographer to a slaughterhouse where pigs were being killed for pork. The film showed people kicking pigs off a truck. Then, the videographer filmed something equally disturbing: It looked as if some of the pigs who were supposed to be killed instantly didn't die right away. CNN is going to air the footage, and they've called Temple for comment.

Earlier this morning, she viewed that video. "Rough handling — there's absolutely no excuse for that. That has to stop!" she tells the TV reporter. As for the pigs who were supposed to be killed instantly, they probably were already dead, she explains. Creepy, but true: sometimes animals (and people) kick or twist for a few minutes after they're dead because their muscles continue to flex.

She ends her phone conversation and turns back to the class. "Not only do animals have emotions," Temple explains, "but emotions drive just about everything an animal does." Understanding these emotions is essential for anyone who lives or works with animals: "If you figure out what emotion is driving a behavior — from a little hen to a gerbil to a horse — you can know how to give the animal a better life."

This is what Temple does for a living: she gives animals better lives. She lectures at kennel clubs. She works with zoos. But most of all, she works with the animals whose milk and eggs and bodies are used for food that people eat. And these chickens, turkeys, cows, and pigs outnumber all the cats and dogs, all the horses, all the animals in zoos in the country *combined*. There are ten billion food animals in the United States alone, most of them birds. Until Temple came along, there were very few effective rules, designs, or procedures to protect any of them from fear and pain on the farm on in the slaughterhouse.

In some cases, that's because people didn't understand what these captive animals were thinking and feeling. Some people believed that animals don't feel fear or pain — and some still don't want to believe it.

"If you ever had a pet," Temple tells the class, "you already know what it took scientists so much effort to prove." People feel fear and pain, joy and curiosity. So why shouldn't animals? Why isn't this obvious?

"Because," says Temple, "animals don't talk." They can't tell us what they're thinking and feeling, so many scientists and philosophers concluded that animals weren't thinking or feeling anything — or that their thoughts and feelings didn't matter.

And that's something Temple understands. As a child, she was in exactly the same position as these animals. Long after other children were speaking in complex sentences, she still couldn't put her thoughts into words. But she certainly could think.

"Autistic people can think the way animals think," Temple writes in one of her books, *Animals in Translation*. Both animals and autistic people experience the world as "a swirling mass of tiny details. We're seeing, hearing, and feeling all the things no one else can. Other people," she later told me, "can't recognize what we're feeling."

"Animals don't think in verbal language," she tells the class. "Their memories and their thoughts are in pictures. Specific individual pictures. Specific individual sounds. A good person's voice. The bad person's voice. The bad piece of equipment they associate with something bad happening, like being chased." Perhaps simpler thoughts than those of most humans, but reasonable ones nonetheless.

"Another thing people don't realize about animals," she says: "they're sensory-based thinkers." They think in sensory images, not in ideas or words. "They're very sensitive to things like high-pitched noises. I can relate to that, too, as a person with autism."

Before Temple explained these things, few people claimed to know how animals feel. And few people claimed to know how autistic people feel, either — because so few of them could describe it. No wonder: if you think in pictures, words are like a different language.

But because Temple learned how to find the words that go with the pictures, she can speak for autistics as well as for animals. She knows both worlds.

"Temple Grandin is arguably the most accomplished and well-known adult with autism in the world," says *Autism Today*, America's largest online autism resource site. Her accomplishments, says Rita Shreffler, the executive director of the National Autism Association, have been "a source of inspiration to parents of children with autism who know their kids have abilities that often go unrealized."

Temple's autism has given her a window into these thinking, feeling minds — a window long shuttered to most ordinary people. But thanks to her, now we can see.

Temple as a toddler.

CHAPTER THREE
WHAT IS AUTISM?

She's retarded! You know it, but you won't admit it!" Temple's father, Richard, yelled at Temple's mom. He was disgusted with their older daughter. When Temple was two, a second daughter, Isabel, was born. Now, at nearly three, Temple had finally begun to laugh. But it wasn't the innocent laughter of a normal toddler, delighted with her discovery of the world. Temple would rip off the lilac-flowered wallpaper in her room, claw through the stuffing of her crib's bunny rabbit–decorated mattress, chew it up, spit it out -- and then erupt in devilish giggles.

"She's not retarded!" Temple's mother, Eustacia, insisted.

"Yes, she is! You just can't face it!"

Temple's parents fought often over Temple. Her father, handsome and temperamental, with wealth inherited from his family, wanted to send her away to a mental institution. Her mother longed to help her but didn't know how.

←————————→

In 1950, when Temple turned three, her mother took her to Children's Hospital in Boston to see a neurologist named Bronson Cruthers, a woman with a "man's name," just like Temple. Dr. Cruthers glued wires to Temple's head to measure the electrical activity in her brain. The test found no damage that would suggest retardation. Temple did not have epilepsy, a brain disease that gives people seizures. When her ears were tested, the equipment found no hearing problems. Dr. Cruthers recommended intensive speech therapy and many hours of teaching.

But it was only later, when the family met with a psychiatrist, that someone gave them a diagnosis for what was wrong with Temple.

"It's autism," the psychiatrist told them. "Infant schizophrenia."

The word "autism" was new when Temple was diagnosed. The term was coined in 1943 by Dr. Leo Kanner, who published a paper in a scientific journal describing eleven children he had studied who were so withdrawn they didn't speak. They seemed to be in a world of their own, repeating bizarre movements, banging their heads, twirling repeatedly. That's why he called the condition "autism": it comes from the Greek word *auto,* which does not mean car, but means "self." Autistic children seemed to be terribly isolated and alone.

Temple's psychiatrist, like most others at the time, thought that autism was a kind of schizophrenia (*skitz-oh-FREE-nee-uh*) — a severe mental illness that causes hallucinations, waking dreams during which the sufferer can't tell the difference between what is real and what is imaginary. And he, like most others, thought autism was caused by cold, unemotional parenting. That theory was made popular in a best-selling book by Bruno Bettelheim, a doctor who had survived a Nazi concentration camp and who thought something awful must have happened to his young autistic patients to make them so withdrawn. (Because he blamed the parents even though it wasn't their fault, some parents nicknamed him "*Brutal* Bettelheim.")

Today doctors and researchers agree that those early ideas about autism were wrong. Brain studies now suggest that autism may be caused by changes in the developing brain that start before a child's first birthday. For some reason no one yet understands, their brains seem to grow exceptionally fast, but at the wrong time. This causes problems in the cortex, the area responsible for sensations like hearing and touch, muscle movement, thought, reasoning, language, and memory, and in areas linking the cortex to other parts of the brain.

Autism is not a kind of schizophrenia. It's what doctors call a "spectrum" of disorders, ranging from a permanent inability to speak or understand language to a handful of what many people would consider mere personality quirks. This latter kind of mild autism is sometimes called Asperger's syndrome after Hans Asperger, the German doctor who first identified it. Many people with Asperger's can be brilliant.

Autism is still very poorly understood. There's still no definitive medical test for the condition: it doesn't show up on a blood test or X-ray (though some changes in the brains of autistics can be seen with the technique known as magnetic resonance imaging, or MRI). Most of the data now show that it affects about 1 in 100 people. For some reason, autism is more common in boys than girls.

Of course, each person with autism is different, just as those who don't have autism are all different. But most people with autism have some traits in common. Their senses can overload easily. Some can't stand fluorescent lights, which flicker at a rate of 120 cycles per second, a rate so fast most that people can't detect the flickering. But many autistics can, and it drives them crazy. Others can't walk down the detergent aisle of the supermarket because the smell just floods their brains. Some can smell the food that was cooked in pots and pans that have long since been emptied and cleaned. Certain sounds can be unbearable: for some kids, the roar of a flushing toilet is so loud that they will wet their pants rather than have to use the toilet and flush it. Rain can sound like gunfire, and noisemakers and fireworks like World War III. Temple knows an autistic woman whose ears are so sensitive, she can hear the radio *even when it's off!* Temple and her colleagues thought this was impossible until the woman started saying things like, "Oh, National Public Radio has a story about lions," and they'd turn on the radio to find the story on lions playing, just as she said.

People with autism often feel overwhelmed by touch as well. Having their hair shampooed may be agony. A hug from a parent can feel unbearably intense. At the same time, many of these kids say they long for human touch. Like many children with autism, Temple used to love to hide beneath the couch cushions. She loved to squeeze into cubbyholes. It made her feel happy, the way a hug makes most of us happy — except *she* was in charge of the timing and pressure of the squeeze.

Kids with autism are prone to temper tantrums. (That was true of the famous blind and deaf women Helen Keller and Laura Bridgman when they were children, before they learned to communicate with sign language. Who can blame them? They, like Temple, were enormously frustrated, and couldn't tell anyone why.) Also like Temple, they focus so intensely on a few favored objects, subjects, or activities that it drives other people nuts. They may talk about one subject endlessly until everyone else is sick of hearing about it, or they may repeat certain activities or phrases over and over. They don't like change.

Finally, people with autism aren't able to read others' expressions or body language well. They might not return a smile, not recognizing it as a friendly greeting. One autistic child went to the teacher to report that another child was "making a strange noise." The teacher went over and found that the "noise" was the other child crying. Even tiny babies

Temple's mother, Eustacia, in a quiet moment before Christmas.

seem to understand that crying means sadness. When one baby starts crying on a plane or in an auditorium, all the other babies are likely to join in, as if in sympathy. But the autistic child doesn't connect the tears and sobbing with sorrow or distress. Temple had trouble reading people's faces, too. She remembers making the surprising discovery that people roll their eyes to signal exasperation and boredom. She was fifty years old.

Dr. Nancy Minshew, director of the Center for Excellence in Autism Research at the University of Pittsburgh, points out that problems like these make it difficult for people with autism to make friends. Even the smartest of these kids, Dr. Minshew says, "are socially and emotionally more delayed than most people ever thought."

But along with these problems, people with autism often have amazing talents. It's as if the brain makes up for deficits in one area with special gifts in others. "Autistic people have a really stellar ability to use the visual parts of the right side of the brain to compensate for problems with language processing," Dr. Minshew says. Most children take a long time to find Waldo hidden in a detailed cartoon — but autistic children usually spot him right away. In situations like this, says Dr. Minshew, autism "may be a decided advantage!" And, these kids may be able to make friends with others who share their interests, such as art, music, computer programming, or writing.

"If I could snap my fingers and be nonautistic," Temple says today, "I wouldn't do it. It's part of who I am." One man, who first heard Temple speak when he was a young soldier stationed in Denver, phoned a call-in radio show years later to talk to her. "Thank you so much," he said, "for giving me the inspiration to say that my brain's not broken. Just different."

But that's not how Temple's father saw it when she was three.

Hearing the doctor's diagnosis, Temple's father again yelled at her mother. "She's insane!" he insisted. "You won't admit it — that's why you won't put her in an institution!"

Temple's mother was adamant: she would *not* send her daughter to an institution. "That would be its own kind of madness!" she said. Instead, she found a speech teacher to work with Temple three times a week. By pronouncing words very carefully, the teacher showed her how to listen for the consonant sounds she had been missing. With the teacher's help, Temple began to hear individual words, and learned to link words with their meanings.

Her mother also hired a nanny, a woman who had previously taken care of a little boy who had problems similar to Temple's. The nanny had taught the boy manners and had helped him learn to talk. She understood that Temple needed images more than words to understand. Sometimes this called for unusual tactics. She taught Temple safety rules by showing her a road-killed squirrel! Pointing to the squashed corpse, the nanny said: "This is why you look both ways before crossing the street — so you don't end up flat like that squirrel."

The world was just starting to make sense to Temple. Her mother thought she might be ready to take a step that many kids with autism at that time were unable to take. Could she ever go to school with normal children?

Autism Disorder: A Few Fast Facts

No one knows the exact cause of autism. There's no one medical test for it and no cure. But one thing's for sure: more children are being diagnosed with autism, and "autism spectrum disorders," than ever before. Again, no one knows why. It may be that there's more autism, or it may be doctors are more aware of it and therefore more likely to diagnose it.

Here are a few quick facts most specialists agree upon:

* Autism usually appears early in childhood. It is not something that develops later in life. On the mild end of the spectrum, a child might be very bright but have underdeveloped social skills.
* Kids with autism usually start speaking later than others and have difficulty using language. Children on the mild end of the spectrum, though, may have no obvious speech delay.
* Most have trouble understanding other people's feelings, are upset by changes in routine, and are supersensitive to how things sound, feel, look, smell, or taste.
* Other common signs of autism include repetitive behaviors, such as flapping the hands, rocking the body, spinning in circles, and repeating words or phrases over and over.
* A person with autism often avoids looking into someone's face and has trouble reading the subtle social signals given by another person's eyes.

* Temper tantrums are common, as are narrow and extremely intense interests, such as dinosaurs, planes, trains, or cartoon characters.
* Autism affects more boys than girls.
* Most scientists agree that genes may cause some of the brain differences of autism. Kids with a brother, sister, or parent with autism or its milder form, Asperger's syndrome, have a higher risk of being autistic.
* Autism disorder is often associated with other medical problems such as gastrointestinal problems, autoimmune disorders, seizures, and allergies.
* Some people with autism are mentally retarded, but some have extremely high IQs. The autism spectrum is a true continuum, ranging from quirky, nerdy, gifted kids to nonverbal people with severe handicaps.
* Though there is no cure for autism, working with special teachers and therapists from an early age can help a child with autism start to talk, communicate, learn, and make friends with others. But older children and adults who lacked early therapy can improve if they have good teachers and are gently encouraged to try new things.

The Grandin family's home on Lowder Street in Dedham, Massachusetts.

CHAPTER FOUR
DIFFERENT BUT HAPPY

Before Temple's first day in kindergarten, the teacher, Mrs. Cole, had a talk with the class about the new girl.

Temple's mom had spoken with the teacher at the small, private Dedham Country Day School, so Mrs. Cole would know what to say. Temple needed help from the other children because there was something wrong with her brain.

It was sort of like polio, the teacher told the class. Temple was born in 1947, a time when American families feared the polio virus almost as much as the atomic bomb. Before the invention of a vaccine to prevent it in 1955, polio struck tens of thousands of children each year, paralyzing its victims and killing many. Everyone in Temple's class had seen children who had survived polio wearing leg braces and walking with crutches.

Temple's problem wasn't something you could see like leg braces, the teacher told the class, because her problem was in her brain. But it was just as real. The children promised to be patient with Temple. And then a shy, serious-looking little girl with brown bangs and hair cut just below her ears stepped into the room.

"First, a girl named Temple — that was weird to start with!" remembers Eleanor Richardson, who later became her best friend. Actually, Temple's first name was Mary, but she hated it. It was too girly — she was a tomboy. Temple was her middle name—a family name on her mother's side—and that was the name she chose for herself, even if other children thought it was strange. ("When we sang 'America the Beautiful,'" remembers Eleanor, "we all used to laugh when we came to the line 'I love thy rocks and rills, I love thy templed hills…'" Temple thought that was pretty funny, too.)

Temple did seem odd. She always called other children by both their first and last names—never just the first, and never a nickname. Sometimes she threw tantrums. Eleanor remembers one that happened right in front of everyone in the assembly hall. Temple lay on the floor and kicked and cried. "The teachers tried to restrain her, while we watched in delighted horror," Eleanor recalls, all these years later. Temple's tantrums were quite the spectacle, she said. "For some kid to do that in school was really something!" One time, when Temple was squirming on the floor during a temper tantrum, she bit Mrs. Deitch, who was in charge of the first three grades, on the leg. Temple was sent home.

The other kids and teachers were mystified by the tantrums. "We didn't know what set her off," Eleanor remembers. "We didn't know what she was thinking."

And that was the source of Temple's frustration: she couldn't tell anyone what she was thinking.

Though she had learned to understand sounds more clearly, Temple still had trouble with some words. Concrete nouns like "house," "dog," and "tree," and verbs like "run," "skate," and "sit" were easy. She could see pictures of these in her head. (Today, even concepts conjure pictures too: "peace" brings to mind a white dove; "honesty," one hand on the Bible, the other hand upraised as in a courtroom, where a person swears to tell the truth.) But abstract concepts don't lend themselves to pictures. As a child, Temple found the Lord's Prayer particularly confusing. "Our Father Who Art in Heaven" made her see an old bearded man in the clouds. But "hallowed be thy name"? What was that about? Was his name "Howard"? At the end of the prayer, "the power and the glory forever" made her see an electrical power line and a rainbow together. But why was there "a men" at the end? What was a man doing there?

Temple had no idea that her mind worked differently from everyone else's. She believed everyone thought in pictures — in fact, she believed this until she was in her forties. She also thought that surely the sound of the school bell hurt everyone's ears and that all the kids suffered from scratchy clothes. And she didn't realize that she was unusually brave about ordinary pain. Once she fell off her bike and cut her knee so badly her mother thought she'd need stitches, but Temple never even cried. "I didn't understand that my senses were different," she says now. "I thought other people were just stronger than me."

Happily, the teachers and children in her class took these oddities in stride. Temple's mother had chosen the school wisely. It was so near that her mother could come to school in a jiffy if Temple needed her. Dedham Country Day School was less than a mile from the Grandin family's stately three-story home, a white house shaded by a big sycamore in front and a huge maple from which a swing hung in the back.

The brick and cinderblock school stood at the heart of seventeen acres of fields and woods. A shady pine grove carpeted with soft needles was perfect for playing Capture the Flag. There were fields for softball and soccer and a lower field that the schoolmaster would flood for winter ice skating. The school was small: there were only nine girls and four boys in Temple's class, compared to the thirty kids per class at the local public school. Parents were deeply involved. There was no school bus, so moms took turns carpooling the children.

With such small class sizes, every child was invited to every birthday party — no one was left out. And because the school ran through sixth grade (today it runs through eighth), most of the kids in Temple's class were together for six or seven years. "We were like family," Eleanor remembers. "Temple was one of us. We didn't question that she needed extra help." Though some kids from other classes occasionally teased her on the playground, "*We* didn't tease Temple. We liked her."

For the most part, Temple's life in elementary school was fun. She loved to make things — and she was good at it. Even before she could ride a bike, she made kites that would fly behind her tricycle. She made parachutes out of scarves. She and Eleanor built a lean-to in the woods behind her friend's house. Temple had lots of friends. Because she was so creative, she was fun to be with. It was easy to overlook her oddities when you were busy working on one of Temple's cool projects.

Her mother remembers Temple's room being "booby-trapped" with her ingenious designs and devices: "Anybody opening the door was instantly entangled by a series of strings crosshatching her room," she says. Two separate red strings lowered and opened the window shades. A yellow string turned on the light. A white string pulled out a sign that read ENTER AT YOUR OWN RISK!

The big white house on Lowder Street was alive with kids: the family eventually grew to include four children, as Temple and her sister were joined by a brother, born in 1953, and another sister, in 1955.

Temple with her baby brother, Dick.

Temple's large room on the second floor, which connected with Isabel's smaller one, soon became a gathering place for neighborhood children. They played table hockey in her room. Her friend Ceelie Beacham remembers four or five kids always being over there. "We'd make up a play and then make the costumes and then call the parents to come watch us," she recalls. "It was lots of fun. Outside, we'd play on her swing set or make a fort or go on a spy mission to watch Mrs. Culver in her garden and then report back."

Temple had various animal playmates as well. To this day she remembers the names of all the neighborhood dogs: not only her own golden retriever, Andy, who liked to follow her on her bike, but also Tucky, the Labrador who loved to chase tennis balls; Teddy, a long-haired corgi, who chased cars; and Rosie, a little dachshund, who sometimes bit people. A large white duck named Wilhelmina often joined the dogs and children at play. Temple's family also had a Siamese cat named Bee Lee and a black and white cat named Bootsie, and Temple had a white mouse named Crusader.

Temple's mother gave her a little sewing machine so she could help

Temple's fourth-grade class photo.

make costumes for school plays. Temple earned money hemming dresses for a local dressmaker. Temple also excelled in art. Her early creations were clumsy, she admits. The teachers always wanted the class to draw people's faces, which Temple didn't like to do. But she loved to draw animals, especially horses. Her friend Eleanor will never forget one of the horses Temple drew. "It was running — it was totally unlike the stupid little horses the rest of us were drawing," she recalls. "I remember thinking, 'That really is cool.' She understood the *spirit* of the horse."

Temple remembers a favorite school assignment from fourth grade.

The history teacher asked the class to try to make Stone Age tools without using any modern materials, not even string. She remembers going to a local cliff to hunt for just the right stone to make the head of a club, then trying to tie the stone to a stick with grass. "It just kind of drooped and then fell off," she remembers. "But I loved doing that. I loved seeing how things physically worked."

Temple also loved carpentry class. All the other girls took crafts, while the boys took carpentry, but Eleanor's and Temple's moms persuaded the school to let their two girls learn to work with hammers and saws. (Today the school lets all the kids take carpentry, which most kids call shop.) Temple still remembers the first project: a plant stand in the shape of a violin, meant to be a centerpiece on a table, cut from pine board with a hand coping saw. Temple later was allowed to use a power saw to make a beautiful model sailboat — alas, she didn't know it needed a keel, so it tipped over the minute she tried to sail it on the brook near her house. (Eleanor remembers her own model boat as a complete disaster. But she still has the stool and bookcase she built in carpentry. When she grew up, Eleanor worked as an organ builder for seven years. "Temple and I both grew up to build things," she notes.)

Back then, though, that future seemed farther away than the clouds in the sky. As graduation from sixth grade approached, the kids in Temple's class tried to imagine what they'd do when they grew up. One girl wanted to be a nurse, another a teacher. Most girls wanted to be mothers eventually. But what about Temple? What would *she* do?

Temple's favorite book in fourth grade had been a book about inventors, with pictures of their inventions: Thomas Edison and his incandescent light bulb, Eli Whitney and his cotton gin, Cyrus McCormick and his mechanical reaper, Elias Howe and his sewing machine. Temple's grandfather was an inventor who had designed an automatic pilot system for airplanes. She thought being an inventor would be a fun job.

But girls weren't supposed to grow up to be inventors then, much less

Temple with kite.

a girl with autism. No one imagined such a future for Temple.

Laurie Gardos, a Dedham classmate who lived on Temple's street, has a picture of Temple from fourth or fifth grade. Laurie now works as a teacher's aide with challenged children. Today, she says, she can see that this picture sums up the person her friend was becoming.

Temple, wearing jeans and a striped shirt, is standing in a field, but she's really in two worlds. Her feet are on the ground, but her mind is in the sky, flying a kite she has built. Unlike the typical four-cornered kite, hers is puffed out like the bell of a jellyfish. But odd as it might seem, her kite is already starting to take off, ready to capture the wind.

Those carefree, kite-flying days were about to end. Junior high school would usher in a whole new set of challenges for Temple. Just as it seemed that her talents were about to take off, changes in her world were brewing, threatening to deflate her spirit and break her heart.

Temple's new school, much larger than her old one, seemed scarily huge.

*etard!"*

    A classmate passing Temple in the hallway on the way to music class sneered. Then the mean girl said it again: "You're nothing but a *retard!"*

Halfway through ninth grade, Temple had just about had enough.

The change from the small, close-knit elementary school to the much larger Beaver Country Day School, a private school just for girls, had been hard for her. The U-shaped brick building seemed monstrously big. There were lots more kids. There had been only thirteen students in Temple's sixth-grade graduating class. In this new school, her class had sixty girls. Adding in the other grades, there were hundreds of kids in the same building. That was hard for a girl with autism to take.

Any change was difficult for Temple, and now there were so many. In elementary school, there was only one teacher in each grade. Now she had a different teacher for each class. And every hour, at the sound of a buzzer (which mercifully was not as loud as the bell in her old school) the students had to change classes. For Temple, so sensitive to light and noise, the echoing hallways, with banging lockers and jostling students, were confusing and traumatic.

It was in the noisy, busy halls that she was teased most often. The words seemed to come out of nowhere:

"Weirdo!"

"Dummy!"

To this day, says Temple, "the words still sting."

Another dreaded teasing zone was the school cafeteria. Temple would gulp her food and then flee to the gym, where the girls who teased her didn't go. There she might play volleyball or Ghost — a game like dodgeball, but if you're hit you can still go behind the lines to catch the other team's ball. She was good at these sports and enjoyed them. But she couldn't always avoid the teasing. Sometimes Temple got so mad she would punch or slap her tormentor, like a much smaller child having a temper tantrum. Today she's ashamed of that.

In elementary school, the teasing was rare, and when it happened, everyone in her own class would stick up for her. This was so much worse. There were so many other girls, many of whom she didn't know.

Most of the girls didn't understand why Temple was different. They just thought she was strange. She liked to repeat words and phrases. (She loved funny words like "Jell-O." She was also entranced by the word "boobs"— not for what it meant, but for how it sounded. She got in trouble for saying it over and over.) She spoke in a flat, loud voice. The strings of words that formed her phrases and sentences didn't always seem connected. Usually, a conversation between two people is like a dance, with a rhythm and music of its own. But Temple couldn't hear that rhythm. (Although she was a strong singer, hitting every note with perfect pitch, she was no good at keeping a beat, singing in time to music, or singing with others.) Her unusual way of speaking made other kids avoid talking with her.

Plus, Temple was no diplomat. A girl who asked, "Do you like my new dress?" might be in for a shock. If Temple didn't like the dress, she wouldn't say, "Well, it's a nice color" or even "I like the one you

Photos from Temple's album from her years at Beaver Country Day School.

wore yesterday better." She might just say, "It makes you look fat!" She didn't realize that such blunt honesty could make someone feel bad. She couldn't read the other girl's facial expressions showing that she felt hurt. At other times, the words just came out all wrong. "In my head, I knew what I wanted to say, but the words never matched my thoughts," she said many years later.

Temple also liked to play pranks that the other girls didn't appreciate. For instance, before class, Temple liked to tie the cords to the venetian blinds to other students' desks. The way she rigged it, when the desk was opened, the blinds fell with a loud crash. It caused a commotion that to this day Temple considers hilarious. During gym, she liked to hide the other girls' clothes so they'd have to go to class wearing their dark blue gym uniforms. (Nobody ever found out that Temple was the one who did it, though. She used to hide her own clothes too, so no one would suspect her. She still giggles at the memory.)

Temple didn't mean to be nasty. She explains today that she pulled these pranks to relieve her boredom. Few subjects at school interested her. She didn't understand math and French because she couldn't make pictures from them in her mind. Most of the other classes were just boring. Her grades were terrible. But making up pranks and watching them unfold made Temple feel like a scientist conducting an experiment. Would the girls have to wear their gym clothes to class? What would the others say? And her "experiments" proved an important point: she might be a "weirdo," but she was no "dummy." Her pranks proved — at least to herself — that she could outsmart the others.

Friends who knew her from the old days, like Ceelie, tried to get the girls at the new school to understand. But some of them just didn't have the patience to deal with Temple. Besides, everyone was much busier now.

The new school assigned a lot more homework. When kids played now, they were more often competing in after-school sports, instead of in friends' backyards. No longer did the neighborhood kids gather in Temple's room to perform plays or make kites together or play table hockey. The girls were interested in things that didn't matter to Temple: they were starting to wear bras, focus on fashion, and talk about boys. One day her friend Ceelie refused to go to school because she thought her hair looked ugly! Her mother made her go anyway.

Temple's mother remembers when her daughter caught sight of herself in a mirror, wearing the shorts she had worn when she was younger, an outfit none of her classmates would be caught dead wearing now. Temple blurted out to her mother, "I don't want to grow up!" Life was changing too fast for her, and Temple couldn't cope.

On that December day in 1961 when the girl called her a retard, Temple exploded. This time she threw her history book — and it hit the girl in the eye. The girl could have been badly hurt or even blinded, though as it turned out, she was fine. But when the girl screamed, Temple just walked away. She didn't even bother to pick up her book.

A few days later, during dinner, the phone rang at the Grandin house. Temple answered the call. She returned to the table pale and shaken. Her mother could see that something was terribly wrong.

"What's the matter?"

Temple didn't try to hide it. She told her family the bad news right away. The headmaster of the school had called to say that she had been expelled from school.

Thinking Differently: Changing Views of Brain Differences

Today ideas about autism, mental illness, and learning disabilities are changing fast. Doctors, parents, and teachers are asking: Should a kid with Asperger's or mild autism be labeled handicapped—or should he be in a gifted and talented program? Do all children who get bored in class need medicine to control "hyperactivity"—or are they just healthy, wiggly kids who need more time on the playground?

Today psychologists have a name for the difficulty some kids have learning to read: it's called dyslexia (*dis-LEX-ee-uh*), and it's considered a learning disorder. But remember, for most of the time that humans have lived on Earth (more than a million years), nobody could read—because writing wasn't invented till 3500 B.C.! Even as recently as 150 years ago, most Americans weren't expected to be able to read. Back when most people lived on family farms, children weren't expected to sit at desks quietly for five to eight hours every day. The kids had to help their parents take care of the animals and plant and harvest food. When they played, they ran around outside. A kid who today would be labeled "hyperactive" might have been applauded in the 1800s for all his energy.

Ideas on what constitutes mental illness have *always* been changing. Before the Civil War gave American slaves their freedom, a physician named Samuel Cartwright published an article in the *New Orleans Medical and Surgical Journal* about a new mental disorder he had discovered:

drapetomania. He invented the word from the Greek word *drapetes,* which means "runaway," and *mania,* which means "madness." This, he said, was the "mental illness" afflicting slaves who attempted to escape from captivity! Cartwright claimed that with proper medical treatment, drapetomania could be prevented—and these captive people would be "restored" to the "healthy" mental state of accepting their enslavement.

Today, doctors have more kinds of medicine than ever before, including some Temple learned about in her thirties that helped quell her constant anxiety, medicines she uses today at extremely low doses. Teachers have developed special classes to help young people with autism and other brain differences learn better in school. At the same time, there is a movement to understand neurodiversity (*NUR-oh-die-VER-city*)—the natural differences in our brains and nervous systems—recognizing that "different" doesn't always mean disabled or disordered.

"There is a tendency among human beings to take people with diagnostic labels and put them as far away as possible," points out Thomas Armstrong, one of the leading advocates of the neurodiversity movement. "A lot of the suffering that individuals with mental disorders go through results from this kind of prejudice." While still offering help to people who have problems with autism, dyslexia, and attention disorders, the neurodiversity movement seeks to uncover—and celebrate—their hidden strengths as well.

Temple was an avid and accomplished skier.

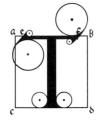emple has set a record!" her father roared. "She's been failing almost every subject, and now she gets kicked out of school! Now you'll have to agree: she should be put away. She can't make it in normal society."

But Temple's mother, who had been researching schools for challenged children, knew there were other roads a person like Temple could take. One of those roads — winding and tree-lined — led to Rindge, New Hampshire.

The sign read HAMPSHIRE COUNTRY SCHOOL. STUDENT POPULATION 32. ELEVATION 1,000 FEET. Here Temple and her mother turned off the dirt road and up a gravel driveway lined with ancient maple trees hung with metal buckets for collecting the sweet sap to boil into syrup. Temple could see horses in one of the snowy fields. She bounced up and down with anticipation.

The boarding school was founded in 1948 by a husband-and-wife team: Henry Patey, a psychologist, and his wife, Adelaide, a teacher, who believed that kids like Temple weren't bad or stupid. Instead, they considered kids like her gifted — in ways that the rest of the world couldn't yet see. Surrounded by 1,700 acres of woods and streams, Hampshire Country School, from its classrooms to its barns to its working dairy, sheep pens, and stable, was created to give these special kids individual attention from a large staff, as well as room to grow. This would be Temple's new home.

"Think Harry Potter and Hogwarts School for Wizards," says Bill Dickerman, the director of admissions as well as a "dorm parent" at the school today. "Until he went to Hogwarts," he continues, "Harry Potter was out of place. Nobody understood him. He was weird. The magic talents he had were scary. But then he found a place where he suddenly was in his world. That's what it's like for the kids here. They're accepted not because of their problems but because of their abilities. And sometimes," he said, "their problems are *part* of their abilities."

When Temple was there, they were kids like Mark Goodman, a tall, strong boy with a special interest in the weather and a love of the outdoors. He wasn't autistic, but he had other problems. When he was fourteen, his parents had him locked up in a mental hospital for eight days. He tested high on IQ tests, but at least one psychiatrist classified him as retarded. Mark was, as he says himself, "eccentric." He explains, "I just couldn't handle cracks in the wall." One day the cracks in the wall of his parents' old home set him off. "I just went berserk over that. I was kicking the walls, slamming doors, and broke my parents' six-inch-tall wedding goblets. They called the police because I was out of control. They handcuffed me and took me to a mental institution. Henry Patey came and picked me up from the mental hospital and took me to Hampshire

Country School." Today Mark is a clinical psychologist and psychophar-macologist (*SY-coe-farm-o-COL-o-gist,* a specialist in drugs to relieve mental illness) with two Ph.D.s, a wife, two kids, a dog, two cats, and a thriving practice in Kansas.

Another student at Temple's school was Jackie Rose, a short, chubby girl with long dark hair who was so withdrawn and depressed, she almost never spoke to anybody. One day when she was ten, with no warning, her parents drove her all the way from New York City to Hampshire Country School and then drove away — leaving her there, the youngest child in the school and one of only nine girls. (Today the school accepts only boys.) After earning a master's degree in social work and another master's in library science, Jackie now manages the youth services at a large public library in Oregon, supports humane charities, and loves to sing soprano in the community chorus.

Mark and Jackie became Temple's friends. Lately they have all gotten back in touch, and they enjoy remembering some of the fun times they shared.

One of the highlights for Temple was designing and building a 300-foot-long ski tow with Mark and three or four other boys. The kids then had to climb for ten minutes or so, dragging their skis up the side of Suicide Hill, which faced east with a view of the campus, just for a two-minute ski down the opposite slope. But thanks to the ski tow, now they could ascend in a jiffy. They all loved skiing down the seventy-foot slope many times each day. Mark and Temple were so proud of their ski tow that they both still keep photos of it in their picture albums.

Mark remembers that Temple was handy with tools and also that she was strong and tough and a fine athlete. On one of the school's many field trips, a group of students hiked up Mt. Washington in New Hampshire's White Mountains — the highest peak in the Northeast. The mountain is famous for having the worst weather in the world because of its unpre-

The ski tow before and after (opposite) renovation.

dictable changes in temperature, dangerous winds, and snow even in summer. In late April, the wind can be so strong it will whip your hat off and freeze your ears. Mark remembers that Temple — the girl who felt tortured by scratchy petticoats — was the only one who didn't complain.

Temple wasn't like the other girls. In Mark's photo album, you can see the difference. In an April 1965 picture, she's standing stiffly, not smiling. The other girls, dressed up in blouses and sweaters, wear their hair long or curled or adorned with barrettes. Temple dressed the same way every day, in well-worn pants and her school jacket, maroon wool with the Hampshire Country School logo in a blue circle on the front. Her hair is cropped at her ears — a very boyish haircut back in the 1960s.

Temple wasn't just a tomboy, Jackie remembers. She was a "Super Tomboy." The other girls liked ballet, plays, music, frilly dresses. Temple liked being outdoors and building things. The other girls, Jackie said,

were "all about teenage stuff"— fascinated with clothes, popular music, and "sneaking off and kissing the boys." Jackie shared Temple's disinterest in kissing boys. They preferred the company of other species. Temple had adopted a dog named Timmy and a barn cat named Stray. When Stray had kittens, Temple gave one to Jackie. Tiger, as Jackie named the little gray and white striped kitten, was her first pet ever. Jackie loved the cat so much, she threw a party for her first birthday. She sent out invitations and made food for the whole school. (At the sight of so many people, Tiger ran out of the room and didn't return till the crowd had left.)

The girls' rooms were on the top floor of an old farmhouse, and Temple constructed cat doors in the windows and doors so all the cats could go outside when they chose. Tiger enjoyed hunting bats and would often bring one, still alive and very upset, back to Jackie's room. Jackie was even more scared than the bat was. "I was petrified. The bat would

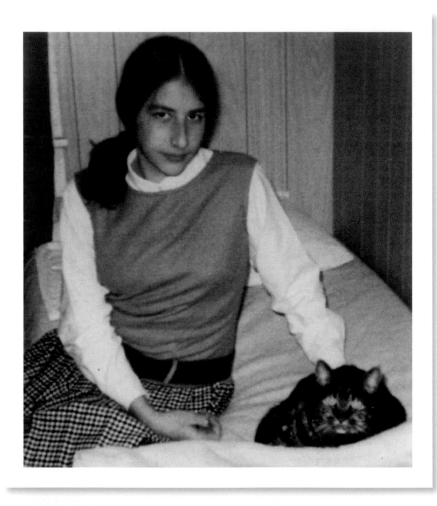

Temple gave her friend Jackie her first pet, whom Jackie named Tiger.

be flying around and I'd scream and put my head under the covers," she remembers. But her best friend, Temple, would always come to her rescue, with a broom to shepherd the bat out the window. "I would be screaming, 'Did you get it yet? *Hurry!*'" Jackie says. "There were many such incidents — until I learned to keep the cat door shut at night."

Jackie's room had a picture window with a beautiful view over the school's vegetable garden and lilac bushes. One night, around eight p.m., she and her roommate, Becky, were looking out the window and saw an incredible sight: a flying saucer!

"In those days," Jackie says, "there was a lot of talk of UFOs. This was pre-Internet. We would read about them, we would hear something on the radio, and we would think about it. What if we saw one?"

When they did, there was no mistaking it: a saucer-shaped space vehicle with glowing lights, hovering right by their window! What else could it be?

"We started screaming 'UFO! UFO!'" Jackie remembers. "The house parents rushed in. We told them, 'Yes, we really saw one!' They didn't

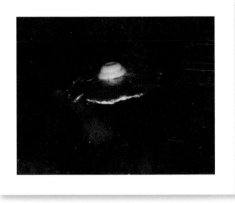

Temple's convincing UFO.

believe us, and we got in trouble. But we would see it again and again — not regularly, but maybe once or twice every couple of months."

Temple, meanwhile, knew exactly what the UFO really was: a translucent plastic Dairy Queen ice cream dish, equipped with a flashlight inside to give it an eerie glow. She dangled it on a string from the roof in front of the girls' window (she had painted the string black, so it wouldn't show at night). Nobody in the school knew about the trick until just before graduation, when Temple came to Jackie and Becky's door with a grin on her face and the contraption in her hands. "What do you think of *this?*" she asked them. (After first pretending to be mad at her, the girls fell to the floor laughing.)

Temple, too, still laughs at that memory. But the memories she treasures most from high school are of the horses. All these years later, she remembers each of them by name. Bay Lady was the horse she rode most of the time: "great in the ring—but halfway on the trail she'd prance and plunge. Otherwise she was the perfect lady." Star couldn't compete in horse shows because she had ankle problems. Circus, a big, gentle horse, died of colic, a digestive disease brought on by eating oat straw. Beauty was gorgeous, but she bit and kicked. Teddy was gentle enough for the littlest kids. King was an old gray horse, so well-mannered that just about anyone could ride him; then you could graduate to riding someone like Flash or Silver. Lady was hot-tempered, and her eyes were wild. "Nobody could ride that horse," Tina Henegar, another schoolmate, remembered. "But Temple could—and beautifully. She was the best."

Temple loved them all and could ride better than anyone.

It's no wonder. Horses, like autistic people, are very sensitive to detail and don't like change. That's why a horse might be frightened of a new white hat, but not a familiar black one—or might panic at the sight of a common object like a wheelbarrow in an unusual place or seen from a different angle. Temple could tell when a horse was starting to get nervous: a fearful horse swishes his tail, and the swishing becomes more rapid with mounting fear. But because Temple also noticed the same details the horses did — like a bale of hay slightly out of place — she could make small changes to calm the animal's fear before it turned to panic.

Temple spent much of her time in the horse barn. She cleaned the stalls. She refilled the feed bins. She cleaned the leather bridles and saddles and other equipment, making repairs if needed. When the farrier came to hammer new shoes onto the horses' hooves, she held the reins and kept the horses calm.

Back at home, Temple's mother wished her daughter would study harder and get better grades instead of riding horses and mending bridles. But Temple was proud that she now had an important, responsible job in the barn. The welfare of nine horses depended largely on her care. To Temple, her academic classes didn't seem to matter half as much. They were "boring, boring, boring."

Soon she began to find it impossible to concentrate on schoolwork anyway. Now in high school, she felt that something new and terrible was happening to her. Her body was changing. The rush of new chemicals her body was producing to change her into a young woman threw Temple's unusual brain into overdrive. She started having panic attacks.

With her palms sweating, heart pounding, and legs wobbling, her mind would be overwhelmed by desperate fear. Anything could set off an attack: Getting a letter (what if it contained bad news?). Not getting a letter (was something wrong at home?). A phone call. Or nothing at all. The feeling was unbearable. "Imagine the worst stage fright you ever had," she said, "but worse. It was like you would feel if you were locked in a room with a cobra."

The attacks grew longer and more frequent. Once an attack started, it might go on all day and all night. Even when Temple wasn't having an attack, she was afraid of having one — afraid of being in public when the tidal wave of fear overcame her, and she wouldn't know what to do.

By the time she was sixteen, Temple was desperate for relief. But who — or what — could ever save her from this assault by her own brain?

Temple loved horses and became an excellent rider.

Temple feels at home with cows, as if surrounded by friends.

CHAPTER SEVEN
"ANIMALS SAVED ME"

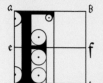lash forward: Temple is middle aged now, but still as supple as a teenager. She gracefully slings one lanky, blue-jeaned leg over the stockyard fence, then the other. Wearing a sleeveless fleece vest over her button-down shirt and a feed cap on her auburn hair, she strides calmly, purposefully, to the middle of the pasture. Then she lies down on her back. She is perfectly at ease. She knows what will happen next.

Slowly, carefully, four dozen thousand-pound steers walk over, forming a circle around her prone body. The huge animals are eager to investigate. "A person lying on the ground is something weird," Temple explains. "As long as you don't move, they'll come up to you." The steers are a little nervous, but they're curious, too. Their furry ears arc forward. They inhale her scent through their wet noses. She can smell their grassy breath. And then one of them extends his long, rough, wet tongue and begins to lick Temple's face. She smiles.

She isn't the least bit frightened lying there, surrounded by fifty thousand pounds of steer. In a situation that would terrify most people, Temple feels completely at peace. That's why she lies down among cattle whenever she gets a chance — whether it's with the herd at Colorado State University or among cows she's visiting on one of her many consulting trips. She has done this alone and in front of television cameras.

She would rather be among the cattle in a stockyard than among human guests at a cocktail party. Sometimes she just can't help herself and kisses a cow right on the nose!

Temple cautions that you need to know what you're doing before you try this. "Better not do this with a bull," she warns. "He might paw you with his hooves." When she lies down among cattle, she's careful to stay still so that they're not alarmed. And she will lie down only in a spacious pasture, not a crowded one. That way, if the cattle are frightened by something — and she knows that a passing shadow, an odd reflection, a coat left on a fence is enough to set off a panic — they won't trample her.

She's sure of it, because she knows exactly what they're feeling.

"I see the world an awful lot like a cow," she says. In fact, she wanted to title one of her memoirs *A Cow's-Eye View*. (The editors made her call it *Thinking in Pictures* instead.)

"I've got the nervous system of a prey animal," Temple explains. Her senses are ratcheted up — attuned to sounds and details that humans don't notice but animals do. She is not blinded to the sensory richness of the world by her ideas about what she expects to see, hear, smell, and feel. Her senses are constantly bringing her information, and she does not screen any of it out. During the terrible, desperate days when she was a teenager, like a prey animal, she was "always looking for danger." This constant state of high-alert is helpful to deer or horses or cattle, who must constantly scan for predators. But to a teenage girl it was torture. Back then, Temple feared she would go mad. She was afraid it would never end. What could rescue her from a lifetime of uncontrollable, unending panic?

The remedy she craved came in the summer of her junior year of high school. It wasn't a pill or an operation; it didn't come from a psychologist or from a course or a self-help group. No, it came from a stockyard. "Animals," she says, "saved me."

<hr/>

It all started half a continent away from her New England home, in a hot, scary, faraway place. Temple didn't want to go there, and even the headmaster at Hampshire Country School, Mr. Patey, advised her not to go. But her mother insisted Temple give the trip a try.

Temple's parents had divorced the year before. Her mother had remarried. While visiting her new husband's sister on her cattle ranch in Arizona, Temple's mom thought maybe this was just what her oldest daughter needed. Strenuous physical activity seemed to calm Temple's panic attacks, at least temporarily. There was plenty of opportunity for that on the ranch. There were horses to ride and fences to fix. And Temple's new aunt and uncle could use her help.

When Temple stepped off the plane in Tucson, "it was hot as an oven," she remembers. *Do people really live here?* she wondered. But it was cooler at the ranch, which was high in the mountains. Temple's aunt, Ann Breechen, put her to work right away.

In no time, Temple had rebuilt the roof on the pump house. She repaired a broken railing on the fence. She even rigged up an ingenious device a person could use to open and close a gate without having to get out of the car. She called it the Magic Gate. All you had to do was pull a rope, which you could reach easily from the driver's-side window, and the gate would swing open. Weights attached to a pulley system would swing the gate shut after your car pulled through.

Temple loved the work at the ranch. She loved riding the horses. She loved watching the big, peaceful cattle. But what intrigued her the most, and fascinated her all summer long, was the cattle chute.

A cattle chute holds a calf still when he or she needs a vaccine or other hands-on treatment. It doesn't look like something a calf would like very

Temple at work making a new gate.

much; it looks rather like the uncomfortable pillory stocks that the Puritans used to publicly punish people. The calf's head sticks out of a hole called the head gate, and the chute operator then pulls a rope to press the side panels inward against the animal's sides. The pressure prevents the calf from wiggling, slipping — or worse, choking in the head gate.

But Temple quickly observed that the squeeze chute had another effect on the cattle. "Going into the chute, the cattle were nervous and twitchy," she explains. She knew just how they felt — she felt nervous and twitchy all the time! But this was the amazing part: moments after the chute was closed, "those nervous cattle calmed right down," she says. "It was almost like magic."

Temple built this "Magic Gate" at the ranch that a driver could open and close without getting out of the car.

Immediately Temple thought, *If such a device can calm nervous cattle, could it help me, too?*

So she tried an experiment. She asked her aunt to close her into the cattle chute. Glancing around to make sure none of the cattle hands saw what they were doing, Aunt Ann reluctantly agreed. Temple got down on hands and knees and put her head through the head gate. Aunt Ann pulled the rope. The wooden sides of the chute squeezed tight against Temple's body.

At first, she felt her panic rising. But she waited. A moment passed, and then it happened. At last, Temple felt engulfed with a feeling of calm, security, and peace — the way you felt as a small child, wrapped in the arms of your mother or father, certain that everything would be all right. Temple stayed in the cattle chute for half an hour. An hour later, she still felt calm and happy.

Throughout that summer, whenever Temple started to feel nervous,

Temple found the cattle chute soothing.

she would go to the cattle chute and ask her aunt to close its wooden sides around her to help her relax.

When Temple returned to school, she set about building a "squeeze machine" in her dorm room out of scrap wood.

Her friend Jackie remembers it well. "I thought it was weirder than heck," she admits. "This thing was made of plywood and sort of V-shaped, and you'd put your head in it. She asked if I could shut her in the machine and then come back and get her a half hour or forty-five minutes later. I would ask, 'Are you *sure* you want me to leave you there?' And she'd say, 'Absolutely, absolutely!' And I would come back and get her out."

When the school psychologist heard about Temple's new machine, he didn't understand it at all. He thought it was strange, the product of a

Before building her first prototype, Temple made this scale model of the squeeze machine.

"sick" mind. Temple remembers the conversation they had in his office. In a looking-down-his-nose, I-know-better-than-you voice, he asked, "We don't have an identity problem, do we? We don't think we're a cow or something, do we?"

"Of course I don't think I'm a cow or something!" Temple answered. "Do *you* think you're a cow?" If only he *had* been a cow! Cattle did more to help Temple than any psychologist ever did.

The psychologist tried to make her give up the squeeze machine. He even convinced Temple's mom it was bad for her. But one important adult stood up for Temple's machine: her favorite teacher, Mr. Carlock, who taught science.

Mr. Carlock ran the school's model rocket club, which Temple had joined. Blue-eyed and soft-spoken, he was patient and kind. He could see that Temple had a fine mind. And here, he saw a chance for her to apply it.

"Let's build a better squeeze machine," Mr. Carlock said to Temple. "Then you can do some scientific experiments. Try it out on other people. Find out if it really can relax them, too!"

And so began Temple Grandin's career.

Temple rode western-style at her aunt's Arizona ranch.

*Temple's room at
Hampshire Country School.*

CHAPTER EIGHT
SCIENTIST AT WORK

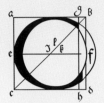'mon, go in. Can't you just get in it for one second?"

Temple's friend Jackie was skeptical. She didn't really want to try the squeeze machine.

"I won't shut you in," Temple urged. "I promise!"

Jackie gave in. Sure, her friend was sometimes odd — but she was also completely trustworthy. Jackie knew Temple wouldn't leave her locked inside the strange contraption. So she got in. She let Temple close the sides. And then...

"I couldn't wait to get out!" she remembers today.

But Temple's friend Tina wasn't afraid at all. She got right down on her hands and knees and put her head through the head gate. Temple pulled the sides shut.

"Do you feel more relaxed?"

"Yeah!" Tina answered. "I like it!"

Temple wrote their reactions down in her notebook. With Mr. Carlock's help, she was conducting her first scientific experiments.

She had to prove that her squeeze machine was a beneficial breakthrough, not the product of a sick mind.

Temple and her machine were caught in the crossfire between two opposing ideas about the treatment of autism. Like many psychologists and psychiatrists at the time, her school psychologist wanted to stamp out Temple's intense focus, or "fixation," on the squeeze machine. Everyone has special interests, but autistic people often take a particular interest to an extreme. They may talk your ear off about the same subject, over and over again. (Jackie remembers Temple talking to her endlessly about science, most of which she didn't understand. "Temple would still

Temple gave a speech at her high school graduation.

be there talking if I hadn't stopped her!" she says now, forty years later.) Ridding Temple of her fixation, the psychologist reasoned, would make her more "normal."

But Mr. Carlock had a different view. Rather than trying to discourage her special interests, the science teacher used her fixation as a motivator.

And he was right. Most experts now agree that an autistic person's especially intense interest can be a powerful incentive to learn, grow, and be inspired to complete even the most difficult and complicated projects.

In order to keep her squeeze machine, Temple would have to prove its worth with experiments. While conducting them, Temple discovered what she wanted to do with her life. She wanted to become a scientist. And she realized that meant she would have to improve her grades, get into college, and earn the highest degree she could.

The girl whose father had wanted to lock her away in a mental institution was now on the road that would lead to her Ph.D.

Temple pored over journals like *Psychological Abstracts* and *Index Medicus* to find the latest scientific papers on her subject. She discovered there was a whole field of scientific study about the senses and how they interact. Suddenly, classes that had been boring seemed interesting—she might glean some nugget of knowledge that could help her improve her squeeze machine.

She graduated second in her class at Hampshire Country School.

She was accepted at a small, friendly college. Like Hampshire Country School, Franklin Pierce College (now Franklin Pierce University) catered to students who might be overwhelmed by classes of hundreds held in auditoriums on a huge campus. Franklin Pierce promised individual attention as well as a beautiful natural setting among mountains, lakes, woods, and meadows. The college was in the same town as her high school, close enough for Temple to visit Mr. Carlock on weekends. In his laboratory, they would modify the squeeze machine, adding foam-padded panels to make it even more comfortable and comforting. The fixation the psychologist had found "strange" and "sick" became the subject of Temple's senior thesis in psychology, testing the sensory effects of the squeeze machine on forty "normal" college students. (Among Temple's results was that 62 percent found the pressure of the machine relaxing—results that she later published in a scientific paper about her studies.)

Temple tested out her squeeze machine on student volunteers.

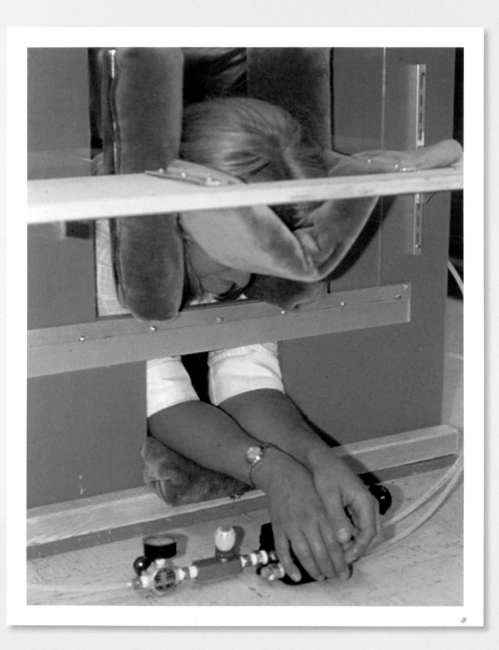

Temple graduated from Franklin Pierce in 1970 with the highest honors, second in a class of four hundred students. From there she went on to Arizona State University to work on a master's in animal science. Her thesis? She wanted to study the behavior of cattle in different types of cattle chutes.

It was a very unusual idea. "Back in 1974, animal-behavior research on farm livestock was a rarity," Temple says. Thirty years ago, students in animal science were writing papers about veterinary practices or animal nutrition. Who ever heard of studying cattle chutes? Nobody guessed that the design of such an ordinary object would affect the animals' behavior—or that it would make a difference to their health and to the productivity of the ranch.

Her animal-science professor told her to forget it. Was she crazy?

But once again, Temple's fixation propelled her: "I was going to do my survey of cattle behavior in cattle chutes even though the professor thought it was stupid!"

Her professor's rejection felt like a door slamming shut in her face. But she was learning quickly to find new doors — hidden doors, trap doors, back doors — that no one else could see, that would open to her alone.

Temple left her professor's office, letting that door close behind her. She walked across campus and through the doors of the university's construction and industrial design departments. These subjects weren't even in the sciences. Yet in these new departments — outside her stated field of study — she found two new professors who would support her.

"An idea that seemed crazy to conservative professors in animal science," she discovered, "seemed perfectly reasonable to a construction man and a designer." The doors she had opened this time would lead to an entirely new field of study, one that would combine design, engineering, construction, psychology, and animal science to help vanquish needless suffering for millions of animals. And it would make Temple Grandin an international success.

When a Door Opens

Temple was daydreaming one Sunday in chapel, a weekly feature of her life at Hampshire Country School. The minister droned on and on. The sermons were usually boring. But suddenly he caught Temple's attention when he rapped his knuckles sharply on the pulpit. "Knock," the preacher said, "and He will answer. 'I am the door: by me if any man enter in, he shall be saved.' Before each of you is a door opening to heaven. Open it and be saved."

The minister was quoting the New Testament book of John, chapter 10, verse 9, in which the door is a symbol for belief in Jesus. But Temple doesn't think in words or ideas. Because she thinks in pictures, she thought, somewhere she would find a door leading to salvation! But where?

She began to look everywhere for the door that would save her. Was it a closet door? The stable door? The door to the main farmhouse? None of these felt right.

Finally she found it. Walking back to her dorm room after dinner, she saw a ladder leaning against the farmhouse, where a small addition was being built. She climbed the ladder to the fourth floor. In the attic of the house, there it was: at the end of a little platform that extended out from the building was a small wooden door that opened onto the roof.

Stepping through that door onto the roof, Temple immediately felt flooded with relief and joy — the same joy, she says, that a cow or a horse feels when he has reached safety. "For me," Temple wrote later, "finding holes and gaps is similar to the way a wary animal surveys new territory to make sure it has safe escape routes and passages, or crosses an open plain that may be full of predators…and when I spot an opening, I get a rush of happy excitement. It is like an antipredator system deep in my brain was activated."

But for Temple, finding that first door was especially momentous. Doors became important symbols for her, marking her many difficult passages and giving her the courage to go forward into new and unknown territory.

Passing through that attic door to the roof and standing beneath a nighttime canopy of stars, Temple felt she had found the door to heaven. It gave her courage she never thought she'd find. That night, she wrote in her diary, "I must conquer my fears and not let them block my way."

The door gave Temple a way to think about her life after high school. "Because I think in pictures," she explained, "I had to relate something in the future back to something concrete, something current. No picture, no thought." Now Temple could picture her future — and envision the steps she'd need to take to attain it.

She passed through her special door many times in high school, whenever she needed confidence and renewal. When she went to college she found secret doors there, too. In a usually locked utility closet at her dorm, she found an eight-rung metal ladder that led to a hatchway opening onto the dorm's flat roof. There she could see a wonderful view of the Franklin Pierce campus and beyond. When she looked north, she could see Mt. Monadnock. Its name, in the Native American Abenaki language, means "the mountain that stands alone." The mountain was sort of like Temple herself: a standout, a peak unlike its surroundings.

Another secret door she found led to the flat, graveled roof of the college library. After her graduation ceremony, Temple passed through that door one last time. There on the library roof, she left a little plaque inscribed with the words *"Saxum, Atrium, Culman"*—her attempt at translating into Latin her new motto: "Strive for the Threshold of the Top."

*At the Scottsdale Feed Yard, Temple observed what made
cattle nervous and what calmed them. They are spooked by
shadows like the ones in this picture.*

CHAPTER NINE
"NO GIRLS ALLOWED"

At the Scottsdale Feed Yard, Temple walked up to the door in the fence that led to the cattle working area. She needed to get in to see how the employees handled the animals in the squeeze chute. She was planning to conduct her graduate research on the cattle much as she had done on her schoolmates in high school and college: she would stand next to the chute with a data sheet and record the behavior of each animal, to see how the design of the chute and the behavior of the operator affected them.

Temple planned to visit many different feed yards, where cattle are driven after their life on pasture to fatten on grain before being sold. The Scottsdale yard was the closest to her dorm at the university, and she planned to do most of her work there. The others were an hour's drive away or more.

She had already secured the manager's permission to visit the yard. He respected her. Sure, she was odd, but she knew her way around cattle. In fact, Temple had written an article for the respected state farm magazine *Arizona Farmer Ranchman* about different kinds of squeeze chutes. The manager was impressed.

But that day he was nowhere in sight. A man named Ron blocked Temple's way as she tried to enter the door.

"No girls allowed!" he growled.

Ron didn't like Temple. He wouldn't have liked her even if she weren't autistic. At the top of his long list of complaints against Temple was that she was a woman. Back in the 1970s, women didn't work in feedlots. That was a man's job. And Temple didn't come from the West but from New England, with her fancy university degree. Ron didn't like this weird foreign woman intruding on territory he considered his own.

So he made a big mistake. He blocked her door.

Ron didn't know it, but at that moment, he guaranteed that Temple would get inside—the next time. By trying to block that door, "he instantly transformed a small, insignificant wood door in a fence into one of my special doors," Temple said. "A blocked door had to be conquered!"

She retreated to her car and sat there fuming. How could she get in? Then she had an idea.

She drove from the feedlot directly to the *Arizona Farmer Ranchman* offices and walked right up to the editor's desk. "I want to write a regular column for you every month," she announced.

The editor signed her on.

He'd been impressed by her article on squeeze chutes. Temple may have seemed odd, with her loud voice and abrupt manner, but her writing was accurate and vivid, full of the sorts of details his readers valued. No one had written about squeeze chutes before. Could the design of something so commonplace really affect the health of a cattle herd? It was an intriguing idea.

The editor was eager for more articles like that one. So he gave Temple what she wanted: a press pass. Now, no matter who manned the door at the Scottsdale Feed Yard — or any feed yard, for that matter — they *had* to let her in.

But that didn't mean they had to be nice to her. When she passed through the door that Ron had blocked, Temple entered a world where she still wasn't always wanted.

Some people welcomed her, like the feedlot manager. Some cattlemen admired her special affection for the cattle. They liked and respected her, and she, in turn, learned a lot from them. She will always remember their kindness.

But she'll also remember the others. Many of the men working with cattle at that time didn't want an autistic person, didn't want a woman, didn't want an easterner, and didn't want someone with a concern for animal welfare poking around in "their" business.

Mike Chabot, general manager of Cargill Meat Solutions, points out that Temple was way ahead of her time. "She was talking about animal behavior and even animal welfare" at a time when many in the industry "thought of the animals only as a source of their products" — not as thinking creatures with feelings like our own.

"You can't believe how hard it was for Temple!" says Jim Uhl. He's the president of Agate Construction Company in Scottsdale. He and his crews have built twenty of Temple's projects in eleven different states. "I remember one guy said, 'I won't have any woman teach *me* how to do cattle facilities!' But Temple has great courage and stamina. She'll hang in there in the toughest situations."

As a graduate student and in her early days as a private consultant, Temple endured harassment that would have cost the men their jobs today. One day at the Scottsdale Feed Yard, she returned to the lot where she'd parked her car and found it covered with bloody flesh. Some of the workers had splattered it with the testicles of freshly castrated cattle. She turned on the windshield wipers and drove home — and came back the next day.

Later, when she visited a meat-processing plant, she was subjected to a "gross-out" tour. She wanted to see how the animals were treated in their last moments of life, so she could figure out if new designs might ensure a faster, easier death. Instead, the plant managers took her to look at the gut truck full of the innards of slaughtered cattle. And they didn't just show her the gross stuff once. *Three times* they led her to the blood pit, where carcasses are hung and the animals' blood drains through a hole in the floor.

Why? "This had nothing to do with humane issues," Temple said. "They just wanted to make me throw up. They wanted to gross me out."

On the third trip, Temple stood in the middle of the deepest, yuckiest pool of blood. *STOMP! STOMP! STOMP!* She stamped her boots over and over, sending blood flying everywhere — including all over the plant manager's clothes.

He didn't dare cross her after that.

Even later in her career, jealous engineers sabotaged Temple's designs. It happened three times in the 1980s, after she had earned her Ph.D. and started her consulting and design business. Temple was shocked; she hadn't yet learned to read human faces and postures, so she had no idea these people didn't like her. Their nastiness seemed to come out of nowhere, and it made no sense. It was simply, to quote one of her favorite TV characters, the Vulcan Mr. Spock of the TV series *Star Trek,* "highly illogical."

"A person who worked for the company got equipment damaged because he was *jealous?*" She is still incredulous today. "It was very difficult to get my head around that — that someone who worked for a company would actually do something bad to their equipment." In one case a jealous engineer jammed a meat hook into a chain conveyor, stopping the system completely. Temple didn't actually see the man do the evil deed. But after the equipment kept jamming, she noticed a meat hook on the floor. She knew the hooks belonged in a different part of the plant. Nobody thought she would see it. But Temple was aware of details other people missed. After that, "another design person and I double-shifted for an entire week to take turns guarding the equipment," she explained. The system ran fine from then on.

In spite of vandalism, gross-out tours, and sabotage, Temple gathered her data patiently, accurately, and in great detail. Her ability to identify with the cattle made her an extraordinarily good observer. "I can put myself into a steer's 1,200-pound body and *feel* the equipment," she said. "When I see someone squeeze an animal too hard in a squeeze chute, it makes me hurt all over."

Some chute designs, she found, actually injured the cattle. No good ranchman wants that. Even if he doesn't care about the individual cows — and, Temple stresses, many ranchers do care deeply — he has to think about profits, and injured animals don't bring in the same money that healthy animals do. Injured or frightened animals gain weight more slowly than healthy, happy animals. Bruised meat can't be sold as human food. All the ranchmen were interested when Temple discovered that some chute designs kept the cattle so calm that vaccinations and even branding could be done so smoothly and easily, the animal was barely stressed. Putting her observations to work could save ranchers money.

This steer is turning away from the human shadow in this picture — Temple's own, created as she snapped this photo.

But it wasn't enough to keep equipment from hurting animals. With her "cow's-eye view," Temple saw that for cattle to have a good life on the ranch they needed more than protection from pain. They needed protection from fear as well. "The single worst thing you can do to an animal," Temple insists, "is to make it feel afraid." Most people would think the other way around — perhaps because we feel we can control our own fears, but not pain. Temple notes, however, that pain is not so important for autistic people. Some will cut themselves, put their hands on a hot stove, bang their heads. Temple hated the feeling of a scratchy hat, but she didn't cry over a badly cut knee. She never complained of the biting cold on ski trips in the mountains. She could take pain. But fear — like the panic attacks she suffered as a teen and young woman — was almost unbearable.

Animals act as if this is true for them, too. You've probably seen this for yourself. Right after being spayed, a dog is usually so unfazed by the operation she'll happily chase a ball the next day. But that same dog, at the sound of an approaching thunderstorm, may go berserk with fear.

In the stockyards, Temple's autistic view of the world lets her see the small details that frighten cattle. Why do they balk and moo when they enter a particular building? Temple can tell at a glance: they don't like that hanging chain — it doesn't seem to belong there and it moves in a scary way. Why won't they go near that one gate? Because someone left his jacket on a nearby fence, and it's flapping in the wind. Why do the cows refuse to enter one building and not another? Because one window casts a pattern of light and shadow on the floor that looks like a hole, and they don't want to fall in. Or a piece of equipment is making a hissing noise, like a dangerous snake. Or the flooring over the threshold is slick, and the cattle are afraid of slipping.

Before Temple came along, cattlemen would often resort to yelling at the cattle and poking them with painful electric prods to force them into a scary situation. That only increased their fear and made things worse. But the men didn't know what else to do. Temple showed them how many problems could be remedied by making small, easy, inexpensive changes. Move a coat, cover a window with cardboard, and miraculously, the cattle would do what the stockmen wanted, voluntarily and calmly.

By the time Temple earned her master's degree, people had started to listen. Her articles in *Arizona Farmer Ranchman* were widely read and admired. She was asked to contribute a chapter to a book on feedlot design.

And then Temple got a lucky break. A door opened *for* her — and changed the fate of farm animals forever.

In her apartment at graduate school, Temple smiles as she reads her first chapter published in a book. Note the hole in her cowboy boot—evidence of hard work.

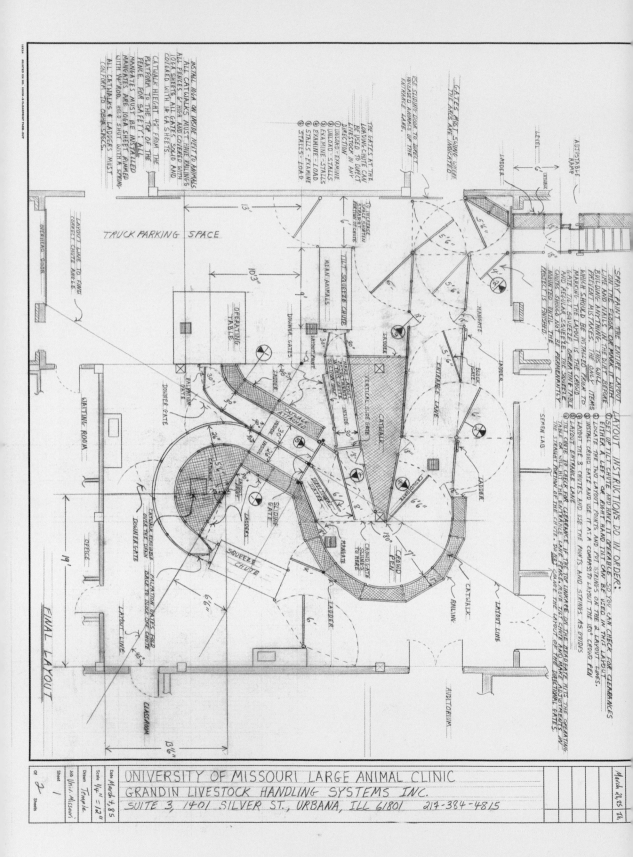

Original hand-drawn design by Temple Grandin.

Opportunity came looking for Temple at a livestock show.

Everyone at the show was admiring the handsome cows and horses on display. But much of the talk among the ranchers that summer wasn't about these beautiful animals but about an ugly little parasite related to ticks and spiders.

Ranchers in Arizona were facing a difficult problem. An outbreak of scabies, a contagious disease caused by mites, was spreading among the cattle. The mites lay eggs, which hatch beneath the animal's skin, creating a terrible, spreading itch. Cattle with lots of mites scratch so hard, they lose their hair, get infections, lose weight, and sometimes even die.

Today, there's a shot to treat scabies, but in the 1970s there was only one way to get rid of the mites. Each animal had to be dipped in a pool of pesticide, called a dip vat. That summer ranchers were building dip vats all over Arizona.

But the cattle didn't want to go in them.

A typical dip-vat pool was seven feet deep. The cattle had to go in over their heads so that even the mites in their ears would be killed—otherwise the surviving mites would just spread all over again. To get to the vat, the cattle had to walk along a steel ramp and then slide down a steep, 45-degree slope into the pool. For reasons no one understood, often the cattle would panic as they entered the dip vat. Sometimes they were so frightened, they would leap into the air, flip over backward, and drown.

Engineers and stockmen had no idea why the cattle were so scared. At the livestock show, one of the managers at Red River Feedyard approached Temple. He had read her articles — maybe *she* could figure it out. He asked her to design a dip vat where the cattle wouldn't drown. He gave her two weeks to come up with the drawings.

"I didn't know anything about dip vats," Temple remembers. Up to that point, she had designed only two other projects: a conveyor system for a plant in Arizona and a stockyard in California. But she knew a lucky break when she saw one. "I call that a door opening. A door's going to open spontaneously and you gotta run through it before it closes!" She went directly from the show to visit some dip vats nearby. She understood immediately what was scaring the cattle so badly. It was the slippery metal ramp.

"Oh, they *hate* that! If I had a calf's hooves, I wouldn't have liked a slippery metal ramp, either. Those cattle must have felt as if they were being forced to jump down an airplane escape slide into the ocean!"

That was the problem, plain and simple. But how to fix it? How could Temple get the cattle to voluntarily walk into the dip vat deep enough to kill even the mites in their ears?

By then Temple had studied, measured, and photographed cattle facilities of all kinds for six years. Her own personal video library — the one in her head — had ideas on file. She ran the images through her autistic mind: a dip vat she'd visited in Yuma, Arizona; another one she'd seen in a magazine; an entrance ramp at a meat-packing plant in Tolleson, Arizona. They all had elements she could use in a new design. She set to work at her drawing board.

She drew an entrance ramp to the vat with a gentler, 25-degree slope.

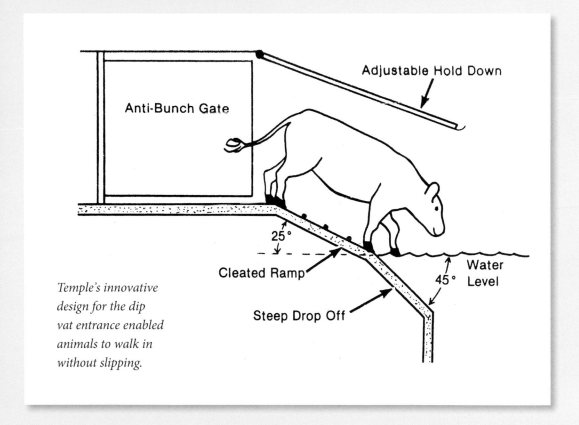

Temple's innovative design for the dip vat entrance enabled animals to walk in without slipping.

She specified a concrete ramp instead of a metal one, with deep grooves to provide sure footing. The cattle would feel safe entering the water gradually, in single file, as they prefer to travel naturally. But they still wouldn't want to go in over their heads. So beneath the pool's surface, Temple angled the ramp steeply to create a drop-off. The cattle would then plop quietly down into the water, over their heads—but then they would bob right back up to the surface before they had a chance to feel frightened. Cattle are good swimmers and would effortlessly swim to the other side. They'd emerge free of parasites and calmly walk away.

———————————————————

Temple's dip-vat design included several other smart innovations. For instance, the platform where the cattle left the vat was usually divided into two pens, so the cattle on one side could dry while the other side was being filled with the cattle awaiting their turn to be dipped. Sometimes the dipped cattle became agitated here. No one knew why. But Temple did. Like children divided from their classmates on a playground, some of the dipped cattle wanted to join their undipped buddies. Temple solved the problem with a solid fence between the two pens. The drying cattle couldn't see the others, so they weren't tempted to try to join them.

Temple knew her design was a breakthrough. With her video-camera mind, she could run the images of the cattle going through it like a movie in her head; she saw that it would work perfectly. So she was shocked—and devastated—when the dip vat was finally built and the cattle entered it for the first time. They began to slip and fall! Two cattle drowned that day.

And then she saw why. The cowboys who ran the vat couldn't believe that the cattle would voluntarily enter it. They were sure the animals would have to be forced down the ramp. So they had ignored her instructions, installing a slippery metal sheet over her nonslip ramp.

As soon as she discovered the metal sheet, Temple made the cowboys take it off. And then, to the cowboys' amazement, the design worked perfectly — just as she knew it would. The cattle walked calmly into the water, submerged completely, and just as calmly walked away. What had been an ordeal so scary that some animals literally died of fright was now a routine and possibly even pleasant event for the cattle. The ranchers had a way to keep their animals healthy without putting their lives at risk.

Building the dip vat.

The new dip vat was such a breakthrough, it was featured in regional and national farm and ranch magazines. Even ranchers overseas contacted Temple. Word began to spread: Temple's designs were positively revolutionary.

Jim Uhl, the president of Agate Construction Company based in

Temple's designs, like this one and the one opposite, include curved paths and alleys with solid sides to keep cattle calm.

Scottsdale, sought out Temple in 1975. He wanted to build cattle-handling facilities, but he had no experience designing them. "There *were* no other designers at that time for livestock facilities," Jim says. "Temple was unique. There is everything right with Temple's designs and nothing wrong!"

The facilities she was creating for cattle were economical and easy to build. But they were designed with more than just the builder's convenience and the owner's costs in mind. Her facilities were especially designed to meet the *animals'* needs — not just for food and water but for something they craved just as much: calm, comfort, and companionship.

Central to many of Temple's innovative designs is her understanding of where cattle want to go: they want to go back home. They like to move in a circle and they want to be among other cattle. They are most

comfortable walking single-file along a curved path. So when ranchers needed to direct cattle into a squeeze chute or dip vat or feedlot, Temple created curved, single-file alleys to let the animals proceed as they would naturally. She designs the alleys with solid sides so that the cattle can't see anything that might frighten them — moving objects, cows going the other way, or people. Instead, they see what is most reassuring: two or three of their fellows right in front of them, proceeding along a curved path to a place they feel is safe.

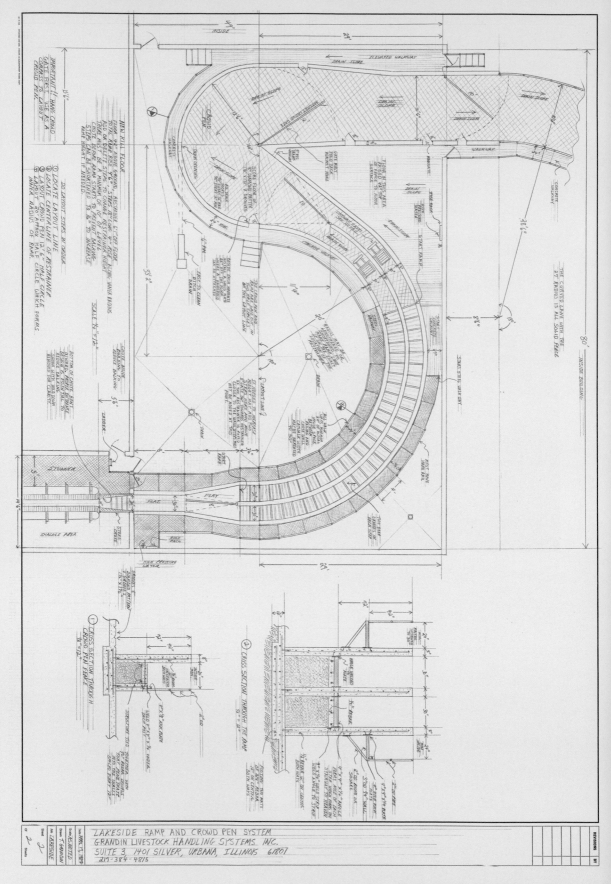

Temple's drawings for this cattle pen reflect the cows' own preferences for walking in circles and following their buddies

In her designs, Temple pays special attention to the details that reinforce a cow's sense of comfort and safety. Each animal can always see at least one or two of his buddies. Flooring materials are always nonslip. Cattle never have to enter a dark building. The lighting inside is carefully modulated so there are no scary-looking shadows. In the facilities Temple designs, there are no sudden noises, no dangling chains, no flapping fabrics.

Temple's "sixth sense" about animals, as her friend Jim calls it, is one of the gifts of her autism. But as he is quick to point out, "It's not just one element" that makes her work great. Along with being brilliant, she's also a very hard worker. "A lot of effort goes into what she does," he says. Over the years they've worked together, he has seen her work seven days a week, sometimes for three months at a time, without a single day off. "We'd always let the guys on our work crew rest up," he said, "but not Temple!" While other facility designers might be content to work with pen and paper alone, she works on whatever needs doing on the work site, "even dragging steel with the guys if it needed to be done. It's the consistency of every day, never giving up, never giving in, overcoming every setback," Jim says.

Some call it focus. Some call it stamina. And some call it "fixation"—one of the hallmarks of autism, something her high school psychologist tried to stamp out. No matter what you call it, one thing's for certain. Temple's commitment is so deep and her devotion so strong that she is willing to face almost anything for the animals.

The Abnormality of Genius

Temple's most important innovations in design were accomplished not in spite of but *because* of her autism. And she thinks that many great achievements of modern civilization were attained thanks to people who may have been on the autistic spectrum, too.

She can name many examples. Nikola Tesla, the inventor and electromagnetic engineer who helped bring the world electricity, thought much the way Temple does. He described how, when he designed electric turbines, he could assemble and operate them in his head as clearly and accurately as if he were watching a movie. Some Chinese mathematical geniuses who could do large calculations in their heads first used an abacus, making calculations by moving rows of beads on a frame. But later they would visualize the abacus to do the numbers in their heads.

Many of the world's greatest innovators might have been dismissed as dummies who had something wrong with them. Vincent Van Gogh, the greatest Dutch painter since Rembrandt, had tantrums as a child and liked to be alone; as a grownup he was so sloppily dressed and blunt that people thought he was crazy. In fact, it's widely agreed today that he did have some sort of mental disorder. Temple points out that the colorful swirls in famous paintings like *The Starry Night* might reflect some of the sensory distortions that autistic people experience. (Mathematicians who analyzed the swirls found that they fit models of water turbulence!) Ludwig Wittgenstein, one of the most influential philosophers of the twentieth century, didn't speak until he was four. Albert Einstein, the founder of modern physics, had speech problems as a child; some people then considered him a dullard. He later told a psychologist friend that he didn't think in words like other people; and, like Temple sifting sand through her fingers, he would be absorbed for hours in thoughts about space and time—thoughts that led to his famous theory of relativity.

In fact, all these people were born with brains quite different from those of normal folks. "Genius," Temple likes to point out, "is *abnormal!*" Does that mean that everyone with an atypical brain should be labeled handicapped? Should genius be "cured"? Should everyone live a typical life?

Temple doesn't think so. "Everybody's not the same," she says, "and thank goodness for that!"

Instead of screaming and thrashing in terror, this calf appears calm and peaceful when handled gently.

CHAPTER ELEVEN
TO HELL AND BACK

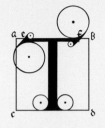emple has endured some awful things in her life. Her father's temper was a terror. In school she endured merciless teasing. As a grownup, she found that her enemies were even crueler.

But even when the feedlot cattlemen trashed her car, even when she was led on a gross-out tour through pools of blood, even when engineers sabotaged her designs — nothing was as bad as what she saw at the Spencer Foods Plant in Spencer, Iowa. She called it "the plant from hell."

It was a kosher slaughterhouse, where food animals were slaughtered according to Jewish law. Ancient rules set forth the special way that the animals to be eaten by Jews should be killed — rules that most scholars agree were originally written so that the animals would not have to suffer. Jews who buy their meat at kosher butchers assume that the animals have been slaughtered in the cleanest, most humane manner possible. But Spencer Foods, and most kosher slaughterhouses in the early 1980s, were doing exactly the opposite.

That's why Temple was there. "I had heard about kosher slaughter, and that it was awful," she says. "I thought I'd go there and see for myself — and then change it." She flew to Iowa and drove to the plant. What she found there, she said, "was even worse than I thought."

Temple describes the scene: "Each terrified animal was forced with an electric prod to run into a small stall. The stall had a slick floor at a 45-degree angle"—exactly the situation that made cattle panic at the dip vat —"and of course the slippery slope makes the steer slip and fall." What happened next was really hideous. With the steer sprawled on the floor, workers attached a heavy metal chain to his rear leg, then hoisted the chain upward so the animal was hanging upside down. Sometimes this broke the back leg, and the animal's full weight hung from the broken limb. But even if the leg wasn't broken, the experience was painful and terrifying.

The purpose of all this was to make the live steer's head point down. Then, a rabbi with a special long knife slit the animal's throat as required by kosher law.

The beast's suffering was over. But right away it was time for another terrified steer to be tortured —and each one knew something horrible was about to happen, because he could hear the screams of the cattle who had gone before. "There was constant bellowing," Temple said, "cattle screaming their heads off. You could hear it in the plant offices. You could hear it in the cafeteria. You could hear it in the parking lot. The workers were used to it."

Why would anyone kill an animal this way? Long before the existence of guns or captive bolt stunners (which fire a metal rod into the brain and kill the animals instantly, the way most cattle are killed today), the quickest way to kill an animal without causing undue pain was to slit his throat. A specially trained person uses a very sharp knife to slice the neck quickly and cleanly. This method of slaughter is specified by both Jewish and Muslim dietary laws even today. Amazingly, Temple says, "when it's done right, the animal doesn't react to the cut. Waving a hand in the animal's face causes a bigger reaction."

But before Temple came on the scene, modern kosher slaughterhouses obeyed the letter of the sacred laws while trashing their humane intent. Poking the cows with electric prods, making them slip and fall, hoisting them upside down to dangle by a broken leg—nothing like that is specified by Jewish law. The only part of the law the system honored was the rabbi slitting the animal's throat.

The rabbis told Temple they hated the system. They weren't cruel men, and they knew the animals suffered terribly. The employees hated it, too. Even those who didn't care about the suffering of the animals hated the process because it was so dangerous for *them*. Many employees wore football helmets, but even so they were often kicked in the head and hurt badly by terrified, thrashing cows.

Just imagine this awful scene—angry rabbis, endangered workers, suffering cattle, blood everywhere—and add the soundtrack of Temple's favorite animals bellowing in pain and fear. No wonder that after her visit, she wrote this in her diary: "If Hell exists, I am in it."

How could she stand it?

Because she had seen even worse.

Early in her career, at a ranch she visited in Arizona, Temple had come upon a little calf who had been attacked by coyotes. The baby, half skinned and partially eaten, was still alive. "Nature can be very harsh," Temple says. "I'm not saying it's cruel, because cruelty entails intent. But a slaughterhouse is *nice* compared to having your hide ripped off."

Temple is often asked how someone who loves animals can witness all this animal suffering. How can an animal lover work for an industry that raises animals to be killed for food? How can she eat a steak when she loves living cattle?

In fact, at one point Temple quit eating steak. She was so sick of all the cruelty she had witnessed on farms and in slaughterhouses that she gave up eating meat altogether. Polls show that 7.3 million Americans are vegetarians, and most of them are very healthy on a meat-free diet (including the author of this book). Another million Americans are vegans, whose diet includes no animal products at all — no eggs or milk or cheese. But when Temple gave up meat, she felt lightheaded and dizzy. She suffers from Ménière's disease, a poorly understood ailment that she feels could be related to her autism. (There might be something different about her metabolism as well as her brain.) When she started eating meat again, she felt better.

"If I had my druthers," Temple says, "people would have evolved as plant-eaters and wouldn't kill animals for food at all. But I don't see the whole human race converting to vegetarianism anytime soon." Ten billion animals in the United States alone, including laying hens, provide food for people each year. What about the quality of all these animals' lives? Don't they matter? By choosing not to eat meat or animal products, a vegetarian or vegan saves thousands of animals from slaughter over the course of his or her lifetime. But Temple points out that if all use of animals for food — including laying hens and milking cows — were eliminated, organic agriculture wouldn't work, because manure from animals is an essential part this method of farming. Besides, 95 percent of Americans do eat meat, and even more eat eggs.

Even if you never eat a hamburger or a pork chop, you'll find animal products everywhere. The thickening agent in Jell-O is made from the boiled bones and hides of cattle and pigs. Heparin, a blood thinner that's used to prevent blood clots, is made from pigs' intestines. Unless the label of a bar of soap specifies otherwise, or says it's kosher, it's almost

Temple's design permits kosher slaughter without hanging the living, panicked cows upside down

certainly made from the fat of slaughtered animals. Even the strictest vegans use animal products in daily life whether they know it, or like it, or not: dyes that color dollar bills, oils that lubricate parts of computers and airplanes, and medicines that save human and animal lives are among the hundreds of common nonfood products made from the bodies of slain animals.

Unless we find alternatives that everyone wants to use, "we're going to have feedlots and slaughterhouses," Temple reasons. "So the question is, what should a humane feedlot and slaughterhouse be like?"

She has seen the answer. "I've seen the ranches and feedlots and meat plants that are really good, where the people treat the animals right. My aunt's ranch. Her neighbor, Singing Valley Ranch. The animals were happy and healthy. They can live better lives on a ranch than most animals live in the wild. And I'd rather die in a good slaughterhouse than be eaten alive by a coyote or a lion!"

This is what helps Temple get through a visit like the one she made to the Spencer slaughterhouse: "I can see how good things *could* be."

Each farm animal deserves a good life, and if it is to be killed, it deserves as good a death as possible. "Many people forget that most farm animals would never have existed at all if people had not bred them," Temple says. She has been criticized for designing slaughterhouses by people who feel animals shouldn't be killed for food — and by those who feel it's a waste of time to care about animals who are going to be killed anyway. "Some people say that since they are going to be killed, being kind to them is not necessary," Temple has written. "My answer is this: What if your grandmother was in the hospital dying? How would you like it if the doctor said, 'She's just a terminal patient. We can throw her over in a corner.'"

Temple believes that food animals deserve a dignified death, free of pain and fear. They shouldn't have to be driven to slaughter by people yelling at them and poking them with electric prods. They shouldn't be forced to slip on slanty floors. They shouldn't need to cry out in fear, frightening the others. Temple designed one slaughterhouse system in which cattle calmly walk up a flight of stairs — which they much prefer to a slippery ramp — to a quick and painless death with a blow to the brain from a captive bolt stunner. She named her system after the 1971 song "The Stairway to Heaven" by the British rock group Led Zeppelin.

But heaven was a long way from what Temple saw at the Spencer Foods Plant. There her stairway system could not be used because kosher law demands that the animals' throats be cut.

Temple drove home and went straight to her drawing board. "I thought, *I've got to get rid of this,*" she says. Right then and there, she started planning a new design without shackles or hoists. She designed a narrow metal stall to hold the steer still in a standing position. A yoke kept the animal's head still, and a belly restraint held the underside snugly. Hydraulic controls position the steer gently and safely. And just so cost wouldn't stand in the way of the new system, Temple gave the drawings to the plant *for free.*

The drawing sat taped to the plant manager's office wall for two years. The management didn't want to bother to change. Finally, though, there was a change of management at the plant. The new managers were eager to adopt the design. Temple returned to work on its construction and was there for its successful start-up.

Temple realizes that horrible abuses of animals continue in both kosher and nonkosher slaughterhouses and on farms around the world. She's concerned not only about her favorite animals, cattle, but also about pigs and sheep and goats and turkeys and chickens. Laying hens, she said, probably have the worst welfare of any farm animal. Because they are birds, they aren't covered by federal humane slaughter laws, which were written specifically for mammals. On most egg factory farms, a laying hen is confined to a cage with other birds that is so cramped, each

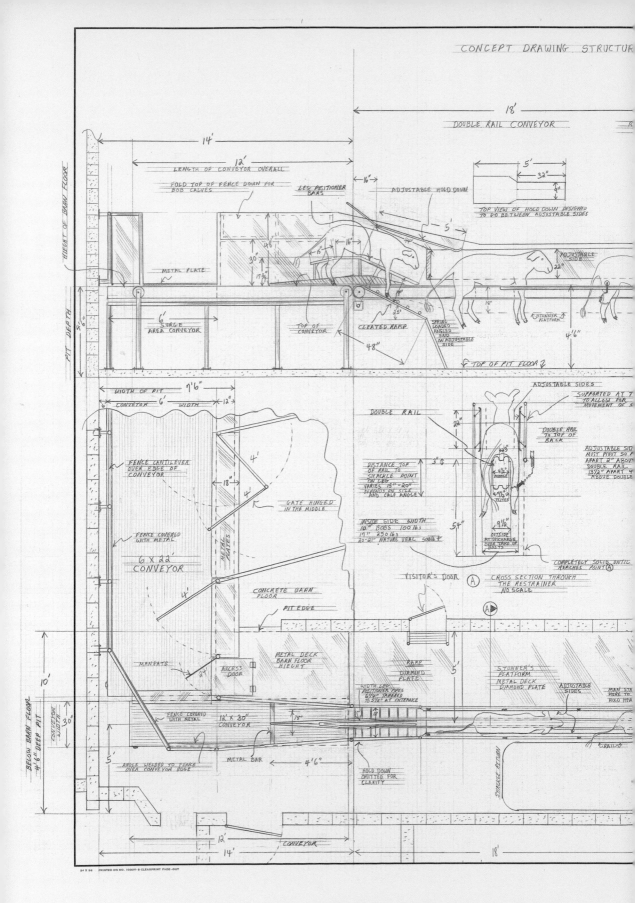

Temple drew these plans to spare animals suffering at a hellish kosher slaughter plant she visited.

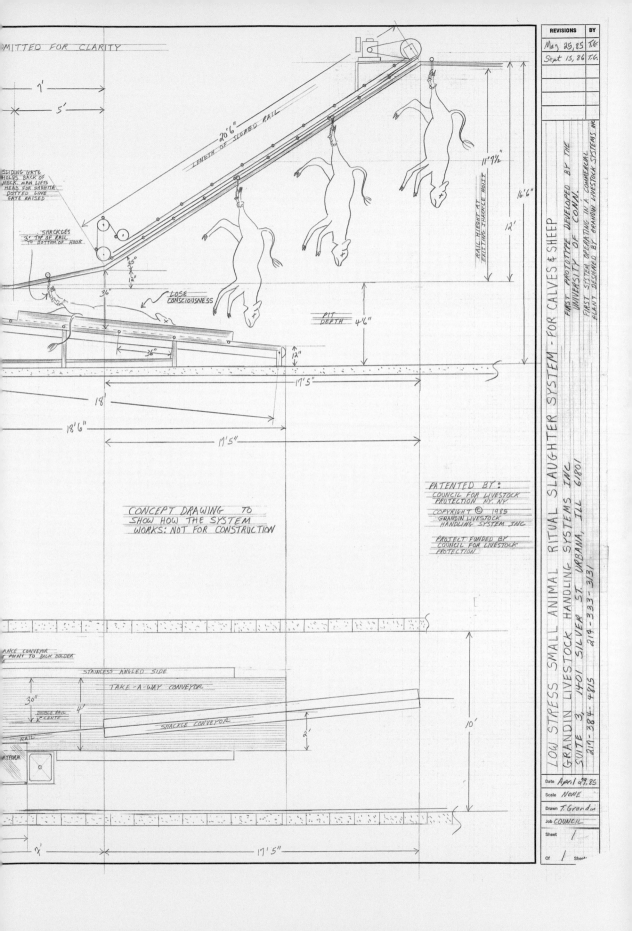

OMITTED FOR CLARITY

20'6"
LENGTH OF SLOPED RAIL

7'
5'

SLIDING GATE
HOLDS BACK OF
NECK, MAN LIFTS
HEAD FOR SHEHITA
DOTTED LINE
GATE RAISED

SHACKLES
3' TOP OF RAIL
TO BOTTOM OF HOOK

35°
12"
36"

LOSE
CONSCIOUSNESS

RAIL HEIGHT AT EXISTING SHACKLE HOIST
11'7½"
16'6"
12'

PIT
DEPTH 4'6"

36"
12"

17'5"
18'
18'6"
17'5"

CONCEPT DRAWING TO
SHOW HOW THE SYSTEM
WORKS: NOT FOR CONSTRUCTION

PATENTED BY:
COUNCIL FOR LIVESTOCK
PROTECTION N.Y. N.Y.

COPYRIGHT © 1985
GRANDIN LIVESTOCK
HANDLING SYSTEM INC

PROJECT FUNDED BY
COUNCIL FOR LIVESTOCK
PROTECTION

RANCE CONVEYOR
POINT TO BACK HOLDER

STAINLESS ANGLED SIDE
TAKE-A-WAY CONVEYOR
SHACKLE CONVEYOR

30"
4'
DOUBLE RAIL
ON CENTER
2'
RAIL
PLATFORM
10'

X'
17'5"

REVISIONS   BY
May 25,85 T.G.
Sept 15, 86 T.G.

LOW STRESS SMALL ANIMAL RITUAL SLAUGHTER SYSTEM - FOR CALVES & SHEEP

FIRST PROTOTYPE DEVELOPED BY THE
UNIVERSITY OF CONN.

FIRST SYSTEM OPERATING IN A COMMERCIAL
PLANT DESIGNED BY GRANDIN LIVESTOCK SYSTEMS INC

GRANDIN LIVESTOCK HANDLING SYSTEMS INC.
SUITE 3, 1401 SILVER ST URBANA, ILL 61801
214-333-3131
214-384-4215

Date April 29, 85
Scale NONE
Drawn T. Grandin
Job COUNCIL
Sheet 1
Of 1 Sheet

bird has less space than a sheet of paper. That's all the room each hen is allowed. She can't even stand up or stretch her wings.

But every improvement in animal welfare is a step forward, and here is a big one: the largest kosher slaughter plants in the United States no longer hang live cattle upside down by one leg—because Temple was willing to go to hell and back for the animals.

Factory Farming by the Numbers

All figures are from the United States Department of Agriculture unless otherwise noted.

* Number of pet dogs, cats, birds, and reptiles combined in the U.S.: 190 million (Source: American Pet Products Association)
* Number of animals raised and killed for meat, eggs, and milk in the U.S.: 10 billion
* Percentage that are birds: 95 percent
* Number of commercial egg-laying hens in the U.S.: 280 million
* Percentage of laying hens confined to "battery cages": 97 percent
* Space allowed for each hen confined in a battery cage, compared to this page: about half
* Number of cattle raised annually for beef in the U.S.: 35 million
* Cows used each year to provide milk in the U.S.: 9 million
* Calves (one per year per dairy cow, a "byproduct" of the dairy industry) slaughtered for veal yearly: 1 million
* Age of a typical cow at slaughter: 3–4 years
* Natural life span of a cow: 20 years (Source: American Veterinary Medical Association)
* Number of pigs slaughtered for meat yearly in the U.S.: 100 million
* Number of pigs kept as breeding mothers on factory farms: 6 million

* Size of gestation crates for each mother pig: 2 feet by 7 feet
* Average age of pig at slaughter: 6 months
* Natural life span of a pig: 14 years (Source: personal observation)
* Percentage of Earth's landmass occupied by livestock raised for human food: 20 percent (Source: United Nations Food and Agriculture Organization. Temple points out that most of this is grazing land not suitable for crops: "When grazing is done correctly it can improve the land. Poorly managed, it will ruin the land. Grazing animals can provide food from land that cannot be used for crops.")

Temple wants to improve life for all farm animals, including pigs, and especially for the pregnant and nursing mothers who are often confined to crates so tiny they can hardly move.

Today Temple is changing her focus away from designing new facilities and toward teaching people how to treat the animals in their care gently and respectfully.

CHAPTER TWELVE
THE OTHER HALF OF
THE SOLUTION

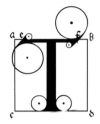emple had spoken clearly, but the restaurant executive almost couldn't believe he had heard her correctly.

"You want us to do *what?*"

"That's right," she told him. "I want you to count moos."

By the late 1990s, prompted by animal welfare organizations, McDonald's had set new standards for treating the animals who became its burgers and McNuggets. The restaurant chain wouldn't buy from a farm or plant that abused animals. But how could they tell if the new standards were working? How to know whether the animals were really being treated humanely?

Obviously, somebody would need to check up on them. Farms and factories that supplied meat to the chain would have to agree to regular audits. But how should an audit be conducted? How do you decide one farm is okay and another should be banished from the buyer's supply list?

Temple was the person the industry turned to for solutions. And, as usual, she came up with an idea nobody had thought of before.

"First, we've got to get rid of unclear standards," Temple told the executive. Standards that aren't clear can't be enforced. Temple gave an example: "'*All animals must have sufficient space.*' This is written in such an unclear manner, it's going to be interpreted differently by different people. How much space is 'sufficient'? You prohibit *excessive prod use.* But what's excessive? You've got to define things! One person might think it's just fine to hit almost every animal with an electric prod!"

Another approach that doesn't work, Temple said, is dictating the exact materials or equipment a farm or plant has to use in every instance. One kind of bedding might be effective and inexpensive in one state but too expensive and not absorbent enough in another. One kind of stall for dairy cattle might be perfect for the hot, dry Southwest but all wrong for dairy cows in New England. One kind of machine might work well on a small farm but not on a big one.

The puzzled executive had to concede that everything Temple was saying was true. But what to do? How to make standards that really make life better for farm animals?

"Let's look at the animals, "said Temple. "Let's look at what they are actually doing and find things we can measure. Like counting moos."

Cows moo and bellow when they're distressed. Pigs squeal. Counting moos or squeals is an excellent measure of whether animals are calm or upset, Temple explained. Her idea was simple: develop a scoring system based on what can be *directly observed* about the animals' welfare.

What percentage of the cattle are mooing or bellowing when they're handled? How many cattle are running when the auditor observes them? (Cattle run when they're afraid; most of the cattle should be moving at a walk or, at most, a trot.) How many animals fall down during handling? (This shows they're terribly frightened or the floor is slippery.

Both problems need to be corrected.) How many get poked with the electric prod? (Most animals will voluntarily go where you want them to if you pay attention to their needs. You don't have to poke them.) How many animals are limping? All of these details are easy to count, Temple pointed out. The scores will be accurate no matter who takes the data. After all, whether a cow is mooing is not a matter of opinion.

"The scores act like speed limits," Temple explained. "Too high a number and you fail." Where to set the limits? When Temple first started developing scoring systems for new meat-packing plants in 1996, she set the passing scores based on what the top 25 percent of plants had achieved. Most of the plants failed — but after a ninety-day waiting period, they were given a second chance to do better. Her scorecards forced the rest of the industry to catch up with the top 25 percent. "And as people get better and better," she says, "you can make the standard even more strict," so fewer and fewer farm animals are frightened or in pain.

Today at plants that supply beef to McDonald's, auditors count moos carefully. Only three cattle out of one hundred can be upset enough to moo in the stunning area. More than that, and the plant fails the audit — and loses an extremely valuable customer.

These days Temple is focusing less on designing new facilities and more on teaching people how to treat the animals in their care. "When I first started out in my career," she says, "I thought I could fix everything with engineering. But you know, engineering can only fix half the problems. The other half is management, and I was very frustrated with that."

As Temple has branched out from helping cattle to investigating the lives of other farm animals, she has discovered monstrous cruelty on some farms. Her first trip to a chicken farm, she said, looked like a Humane Society undercover video. Right in front of her — and in front of a vice president from McDonald's — workers were loading chickens on their way to slaughter into coops by picking them up by one wing, snapping the bones in two. Live chickens were run over with forklifts.

Temple (far right) and her colleagues look dressed for space flight, but they're wearing "moon suits" to protect the animals from human germs during an inspection for McDonald's.

At the farm's hatchery, they saw a box filled with half-dead babies, who were going to be thrown into the garbage alive. At another chicken farm, hens were packed in cages so tightly that they were on top of each other. The older hens were half bald. They were so distressed in their tiny, dirty cages that they had rubbed, picked, or beaten their feathers off.

When Temple confronted the manager at one of the farms with what she had seen, he replied, "There's nothing wrong with my birds. They've got good health. I take good care of my birds."

Cruelty had been tolerated for so long on this farm that "bad" had become the new normal. And if the management doesn't care about animal welfare, workers follow suit.

When Temple sat down with the vice president of the company that bought eggs from the farm later that same day, she told him about her

Temple looks in on chickens who have much more space than most hens who provide eggs for supermarkets and restaurants do.

"ten-people-from-the-airport rule." It goes like this: "If I brought ten random people from the airport out to this chicken farm, would they say the hens are getting good care? Would they say they're in decent conditions, where they don't experience mental or physical anguish? Or would they say this is cruel and inhumane treatment of innocent animals?"

The vice president of the egg company called her the next day. "You made me do some thinking," he said. He gave his hens more space.

"I think we have to look at everything we do on farms this way," Temple insists. "What would ten random people from the airport think if they saw this? What if you brought your wedding guests to this farm or packing plant? What would they think? Are you going to be proud to show them your animals — or are you going to be squirming?"

In fact, some widely accepted practices on America's large commercial farms would flunk her test. One year Temple conducted her own survey during the many flights she takes to and from her speaking engagements. She showed the people sitting next to her pictures of mother pigs on typical pork farms. The mother pigs are forced to live in gestation stalls so small that these intelligent, affectionate animals can't even turn around. "Two thirds of the people I asked hate gestation stalls," she found. "As soon as they find out the pigs can't turn around, they say *nah!*" Temple's informal survey results exactly matched those of a survey conducted in 2010 in Ohio. Under pressure from humane groups, the state farm bureau has now agreed to phase out gestation stalls there.

Temple can't take millions of Americans to see the farms and plants where our food animals live and die. So she's doing the next best thing: she's putting video cameras in barns, feedlots, and even slaughterhouses. In some cases, only the farm manager sees the videos. In other cases, auditors are able to watch them at any time, so that bad farmers can't fake good behavior when the auditor shows up at the door. And in a few cases, anyone can see the videos — on the Internet.

"Farms and slaughterhouses should have glass walls," Temple wrote in her 2009 book, *Animals Make Us Human*. "People need to see what's happening on farms and inside plants!"

When she first suggested the idea of videos and webcams, though, some people in the industry went berserk. Temple remembers their reaction: "They thought I was off my rocker."

She has heard that one before. People have been calling Temple Grandin "crazy," "retarded," and "off her rocker" ever since her father first insisted she be put away in an institution when she was three years old.

She's proved them wrong every time.

CHAPTER THIRTEEN
TEMPLE TODAY

As you enter the foyer of the condo where Temple lives in Fort Collins, Colorado, the first thing you notice is the wall by the stairway. It's lined from floor to ceiling with plaques, mementos, and awards. The framed covers of all her books hang here, along with the back of the director's chair from the HBO TV movie about her life. Along the wall, marching upstairs to the second floor, are awards from such organizations as the Humane Society and even the Beef Council — awards for her designs, her books, and her actions on behalf of animals and fellow autistics.

All this looks very professional and grown-up. But the living room is where Temple keeps the fun stuff. The mantel above the white brick fireplace is lined with animal figurines. Each one has a story. "This pig is from Denmark, when I visited there," she says, picking up a smiling pink porcelain figure.

"This sheep is from Australia. Here's a cow — it's from Chicago. The cowbell here, this came from Switzerland..." The centerpiece of the living room is a coffee table, but there's not much room on it for coffee. It, too, is piled high with treasures: a pig keychain that grunts and lights up when you push a button; a porcelain cow cream pitcher with a hole in the mouth where you can pour cream out; a plastic model draft horse with movable legs. The most prominent of the figures is a two-foot-tall horse sculpture made of leather. It was a gift from the film star Claire Danes, who played Temple in the TV movie.

Here, in her cozy home, is Temple's life made visible. Her downstairs office is piled high with books and magazines she's reading on animals and autism and design. Her upstairs office is covered with hundreds of

Awards for engineering, writing, and speaking line the wall of Temple's stairway.

badges and press passes, many with colorful ribbons, from conferences, conventions, and livestock shows she's attended. Some date all the way back to her graduate school days, when she worked as a columnist for *Arizona Farmer Ranchman*. They cover the curtains by the window so completely, you can't even tell the color of the curtain fabric.

Likewise, it's hard to see yourself in any of her mirrors. The ones over the bureau and in the bathroom are almost completely covered with sticky tabs and scraps of paper held in place with tape — all reminders of her extensive To Do list. For Temple, mirrors aren't all that important. She doesn't really need to look at her reflection. She would rather look at her life.

All the press passes and plaques, all the figurines and knickknacks, are physical evidence of the memories in her head. That's why Temple keeps them all. "Every one of these things," she explains, "is a tangible reminder of things that I did."

Many of her accomplishments were achieved in spite of her autism. The people who gather to hear her at conferences are astonished when this poised, confident, accomplished woman tells them, "When I was a little kid, I had all the full-blown symptoms of autism. I had no language. I had tantrums. I would just sit and rock…"

Though many of these symptoms are gone, Temple is still autistic, still facing the same issues that people with autism battle every day. She still

has trouble with loud noises. She jumps when a car backfires, and she hates the roar of motorcycles and the sound of a TV yammering in the background at a restaurant. She avoids places like sports bars because they're so loud.

She broke off one talk to an autism group at a Sheraton Hotel ballroom because of a low hum coming from the hallway in back of her podium. She strode into the hallway and found a hotel employee. Because her microphone was still clipped to her shirt, everyone in the audience could hear what she said to him. "*What* is making that terrible noise?" she demanded. "It's driving us crazy! Maybe you could unplug it."

The noise stopped. As Temple reentered the room, like a knight who had just slain a dragon, she announced, "It was a half-dead, empty Coca-Cola cooler." The audience — autistic people and their parents and caregivers — erupted into applause.

Temple has not gotten rid of autism. Autism does not go away. Her signature button-down cowboy shirts would feel unbearable if she didn't put them on over a well-worn T-shirt to soften the itch. She never wears dresses, because she can't stand the feel of her legs rubbing together. She washes new underclothes many times to make them soft enough to wear.

She still has trouble hearing certain words correctly. To her, "woodchuck" sounds like "workshop," "therefore" sounds like "air force," and "doormat" sounds like "floor lamp." She can usually figure out what people are saying, though, from the context in which the words appear. "If I'm at work on a design project, I know the engineer probably is talking about a workshop instead of a woodchuck!" she says.

Thankfully, the constant sense of panic that dogged her as a teenager is now gone. She takes very small doses of antidepressants to deal with that feeling.

Many of the other problems of autism she has simply learned to cope with over the years. Temple has dramatically altered the way she speaks by watching videos of her talks and revising her tone to sound more like a typical person talking. ("It would have been better to spend more time with speech therapists and less with psychologists when I was growing up," she now says.) She has even learned, "almost like an actress learning a script," how to make small talk with people. She confines her chitchat to three topics: the weather, pets, and travel. (Especially travel *problems* — if you ask Temple to tell you about "the world's worst vomit flights," both of you will be overcome with laughter at her tale of the poor guy who "managed to throw up on a full third of the coach section" during the first twenty minutes of a four-hour flight from New York to Phoenix.) She stays away from sex, politics, and religion.

The emotions of typical humans are still a mystery to her. She "doesn't get" *Romeo and Juliet*. She can't understand why other people are so interested in soap operas and romance novels and movies in the "drama" category. (She likes sci-fi, animals, and action films — she loved *Babe*, *Wallace & Gromit*, and the *Star Trek* movies.)

Reading people's expressions and understanding their body language still doesn't come naturally. From the image library in her brain, Temple assembled a sort of field guide to help her see that crossed arms and a frowning mouth might signal a jealous engineer, or that rolling eyes may mean that a student doesn't believe her. Temple told the neurologist and author Oliver Sacks that most of the time, among her fellow humans, she feels like "an anthropologist on Mars."

But all that is fine with her. Temple doesn't want a brain like most other people have.

"A lot of normal people are fuzzy in their thinking," she says. She was horrified to learn, in her forties, that the images in other people's minds are often just generalized ideas of a church steeple or a dog or a shoe — not the specific, detailed images she enjoys when she thinks. To her, that's a disability, like that of a person who can't see or hear clearly. "I like the way I think," she says. Autism gave her the gift of "the ultimate virtual-reality system," the ability to see accurate, distinct pictures and to manipulate them in her head. Thanks to her autism, she is able to put herself inside the emotional and sensory system of a cow or a horse or a pig, to dwell in the world of animals and know, as few others can, what they think and feel. Autism gave her these special skills. "Autism," she says, "is part of who I am."

← — — — — — — — — →

Temple has made for herself an unusual life. She doesn't have many of the things most people think they need: a spouse, kids of her own, a big, expensive house, a closetful of fancy clothes. She doesn't need them. What she does have is far more important: a life rich and full of meaning. "When I get to do something to improve treatment of animals, when I get to help a mother with her autistic kid, when I help one of my students get a good career…" Temple pauses. "Well, that's the meaning of life for me. It's that simple."

A picture of one of her heroes, Albert Einstein, watches over Temple's small bed. Beneath the black-and-white photo of the wild-haired physicist appears this quote: "The Ideals which have lighted my way, and time after time have given me new courage to face life cheerfully, have been kindness, beauty and truth."

Next to Temple's bed sits her squeeze machine. It's been improved many times since her high school years. Now it boasts finer controls and more padding. It's painted her favorite colors, yellow and blue. For many years she used it at least once a week, closing it tight around her for half an hour. But today it's covered with dust. She hasn't used it since the pneumatic controls broke a year or so ago. She explains she just hasn't had time to fix it. Besides, she says, "I'm getting into hugging people now."

APPENDIX
TEMPLE'S ADVICE FOR
KIDS ON THE SPECTRUM

1. *Geek out!* "Though I was socially awkward, I had friends who shared my interests," Temple says. "Get into different clubs. The Lego-Mindstorm-Robotics Club, the Computer Club, the Drama Club, the Art Club." It's easier to make friends with other kids when you're working together on cool projects that show your skills.

2. *Work for others.* "I'm seeing too many kids on the autism spectrum who are smart and creative but have never had a job walking a dog or delivering a newspaper," she says. "To get on in the real world, you've got to learn to do a task for somebody else." It's essential to learn basic hygiene and manners, too, so that other people will get along with you.

3. *Develop a portfolio.* Whether you want to be an editor of your school yearbook or are going for a job interview, show people your work. "When I started out in the industry, people thought I was really weird and didn't want to talk with me," Temple says. "Then I showed them my drawings. That changed the attitude." Keep a portfolio with examples of your photography, or articles you've written, photos of the model rockets you've built, clothing you've sewn. "One of the things I learned to be successful is to sell my work and not myself. How did I convince big companies to use my designs?

I sent them drawings, pictures of other jobs, articles I had written in cattle magazines. I didn't give them huge file folders and blobs of other stuff — just enough so they'd open it up and look at it for fifteen seconds, and it's *wow*."

4. *Find someone who can open the door for you.* It might be a teacher like Mr. Carlock, a clergyperson, or a friend's mom or dad. When you are older, it might be a professor outside your chosen field of study, as it was for Temple in grad school — or it might be someone like her editor at *Arizona Farmer Ranchman*. "A lot of quirky kids try to do a regular job interview, and they're done for," Temple says. "They've got to short-circuit that process. I never got a job through a regular job interview. Never. I was not showing my portfolio to the job-interview person, I was showing it to the engineering department. So get to the right person."

5. *Focus on your strengths.* "There's too much emphasis on the deficit and not enough emphasis on building up the area of strength." Temple worries that schools are cutting programs in the sorts of things she was good at like art, carpentry, welding, and drafting. If your school doesn't offer classes in the subjects you enjoy, try to find another way to pursue them, perhaps a class outside school or even an internship or a job with a grownup.

6. *Have faith.* There is more to life than social interactions, even if most of the people around you don't realize it. "The world is so socially attuned," Temple says, "but you wouldn't have any comput-

ers or any electricity or anything if it weren't for those techie people who are not so socially attuned. There's a whole cool techie world out there." Society desperately needs the skills you have, to invent new computer applications, to make engineering breakthroughs, to make the next big discoveries in physics or medicine — or whatever your area of interest.

7. *Sometimes you just have to do it.* "One way to get things done is, don't always wait for permission," says Temple. "Just do it! If you ask permission for every little thing, you'll never get anything done." Be inventive. Find a new way no one has thought of and make it work. Then show off the finished product and let it speak for itself. Don't give anyone a chance to block that door.

SELECTED BIBLIOGRAPHY AND RESOURCES

The following books, articles, films, and websites were used in the research for this book. Also included are resources Temple recommends for kids, teachers, and parents.

BOOKS

Armstrong, Thomas. *Neurodiversity: Discovering the Extraordinary Gifts of Autism, ADHD, Dyslexia and Other Brain Differences.* Boston: DaCapo Lifelong Books, 2010.

Cutler, Eustacia. *A Thorn in My Pocket: Temple Grandin's Mother Tells the Family Story.* Arlington, Tex.: Future Horizons, 2004.

Grandin, Temple. *Thinking in Pictures and Other Reports from My Life with Autism.* New York: Random House, 1995.

———. *The Way I See It.* Arlington, Tex.: Future Horizons, 2007.

Grandin, Temple, and Kate Duffy. *Developing Talents: Careers for Individuals with Asperger Syndrome and High-Functioning Autism.* Shawnee Mission, Kans.: Autism Asperger Publishing Company, 2008.

Grandin, Temple, and Catherine Johnson. *Animals in Translation: Using the Mysteries of Autism to Decode Animal Behavior.* New York: Scribner, 2005.

———. *Animals Make Us Human: Creating the Best Life for Animals.* Boston: Houghton Mifflin Harcourt, 2009.

Grandin, Temple, and Margaret M. Scariano. *Emergence: Labeled Autistic.* New York: Warner Books, 1986.

Isaacson, Rupert. *The Horse Boy.* New York: Back Bay Books, 2009.

Ledgin, Norm. *Asperger's and Self-Esteem: Insight and Hope Through Famous Role Models.* Arlington, Tex.: Future Horizons, 2002.

Sacks, Oliver. *An Anthropologist on Mars.* New York: Knopf, 1995.

Volkmar, Fred R., and Rhea Paul, Ami Klin, and Donald Cohen, eds. *Handbook of Autism and Pervasive Developmental Disorders.* Vol. 2. Hoboken, N.J.: John Wiley and Sons, 2005.

ARTICLES

Grandin, Temple. "Calming Effects of Deep Touch Pressure in Patients with Autistic Disorder, College Students, and Animals." *Journal of Child and Adolescent Psychopharmacology* 2 (1992): 63–72.

———. "Assessment of Stress During Handling and Transport." *Journal of Animal Science* 75 (1997): 249–57.

———. "Effect of Animal Welfare Audits of Slaughter Plans by a Major Fast Food Company on Cattle Handling and Stunning Practices." *Journal of the American Veterinary Medical Association* 216 (2000): 848–51.

———. "Cattle Vocalizations Are Associated with Handling and

Equipment Problems at Beef Slaughter Plants." *Applied Animal Behavior Science* 71 (2001): 191–201.

———. "Animals Are Not Things: A View on Animal Welfare Based on Neurological Complexity." In *People, Property and Pets.* Ed. Marc Hauser, Fiery Cushman, and Matthew Kamen. Lafayette, Ind.: Purdue University Press, 2006.

Sacks, Oliver. "A Neurologist's Notebook: An Anthropologist on Mars." *The New Yorker,* Dec. 17, 1993–Jan. 3, 1994, 106–25.

WEBSITES

www.templegrandin.com Temple's website has detailed information about both autism and animal welfare. Check out the great videos of animal-handling techniques.

www.grandin.com Lots of information about Temple's work with livestock, including diagrams and photos of her curving cattle-chute designs.

www.cdc.gov/ncddd/autism/index.html The Center for Disease Control's Autism Spectrum Disorder page.

www.autismtoday.com The largest online service for news on autism research, resources, and books.

www.autism-society.org The oldest national autism group.

www.autism.com Discusses autism treatments.

www.autismspeaks.org The organization funds research on autism and publishes results of research studies.

www.pittautismresearch.org Based at the University of Pittsburgh, the Center for Excellence in Autism Research is dedicated to understanding the nature of autism. It coordinates autism research sponsored by the National Institute of Health at five institutions.

www.nationalautismassociation.org Advocates for, educates, and empowers those affected by autism.

www.wrongplanet.net Online community and resource for autism and Asperger's. This site is run by a person on the autism spectrum and has writings and videos by others on the spectrum.

www.nebi.rlm.nih.gov/pubmed A searchable database of medical journal articles.

www.ted.com/talks/lang/eng/temple_grandin_the_world_needs_all_ kinds_of_minds.html Temple speaks on the gifts that autism has brought to her and the world.

www.humanesociety.org The Humane Society of the United States is the nation's oldest and largest animal welfare organization.

www.americanhumane.org The American Humane Association. A leader in identifying and preventing the causes of animal and child abuse and neglect.

www.awionline.org The Animal Welfare Institute. A charity formed to reduce the pain and fear people inflict on animals.

www.certifiedhumane.org Certified Humane. This nonprofit was created to improve the lives of farm animals by setting humane standards and conducting inspections on farms and in slaughterhouses.

www.ufaw.org.uk Universities Federation for Animal Welfare, based in the United Kingdom. Uses scientific knowledge to improve welfare of animals as pets, in zoos, on farms, in laboratories, and in the wild.

www.wspa_international.org World Society for the Protection of Animals. An international alliance of animal welfare groups.

www.ucsusa.org/assets/documents/food_and_agriculture/cafos-uncovered.pdf A good overview article on factory farms by the Union of Concerned Scientists.

www.animalhandling.org Contains Temple Grandin's Recommended Animal Handling Guidelines and Audit Guide. This is the scoring system used by McDonald's and other companies to audit slaughter plants.

www.meatami.com The American Meat Institute (AMI) is the oldest and largest trade organization representing the meat and poultry trades.

FILMS

Temple Grandin, HBO Films, 2010.

The Woman Who Thinks Like a Cow, BBC Horizon Films, 2006.

"Stairway to Heaven," episode of *First Person* documentary TV series, 1998.

ACKNOWLEDGMENTS

My thanks to the many people who helped me while I researched and wrote this book. I am especially grateful to Amy Markus, director of the town library in Hancock, New Hampshire, and, during the early phase of my research, my personal assistant; Julie Hagan and Ashley Linell of Dedham Country Day School; Bill Dickerman of Hampshire Country School; Temple's childhood and high school friends Ceelie Beacham, Laurie Gardos, Eleanor Richardson, Mark Goodman, Jackie Rose, and Tina Henegar; Amanda Borozinsky and Bob LaFlamme at Franklin Pierce University; Jim Uhl, president and CEO of Agate Construction Company; the faculty and staff at Colorado State University's Department of Animal Science, who welcomed me to many classes there; Temple's cheerful and able assistant, Cheryl Miller; Selinda Chiquoine, Robert and Judith Oksner, Howard Mansfield, Gretchen Morin, Elizabeth Marshall Thomas, Jody Simpson, Steven Wise, and Siena Wise, who read and helped revise early drafts of the manuscript; Sue Ingalls, an extraordinary teacher who shared with me her experience with an autistic student; my literary agent and friend, Sarah Jane Freymann; my treasured editor at Houghton Mifflin Harcourt, Kate O'Sullivan; book designer, Cara Llewellyn; and Betsy Groban of Houghton Mifflin Harcourt, who first suggested the idea for this book. Thank you to Hal and Kerry Adams for a lovely morning with their Holsteins at Black Brook

Farm, where the photo of Temple and me on the book's back flap was taken.

A special note of thanks goes to Temple's extraordinary mother, Eustacia Cutler, who stuck up for her daughter, stood by her, taught her, found special therapists and tutors, and believed in her talents. Temple will be forever grateful to her mom — and I am, too. Temple and Eustacia sometimes share a podium and lecture on autism together; Eustacia stood by Temple's side at the glamorous Emmy Awards ceremony when the movie on Temple's life won award after award in 2010. Eustacia's wonderful book from a mother's perspective is a great source of information and inspiration for mothers everywhere.

Most of all I thank Temple Grandin, for welcoming me to her home and workplace with patience, kindness, openness, and friendship. Thank you, Temple, for your example of how to use your life's unique gifts to help both animals and people.

Temple and her mother celebrated together at the Emmy Awards as the biopic of Temple's life was honored again and again.

PHOTO CREDITS

All images and design drawings courtesy of
Temple Grandin except the following:

* Cowhide background images courtesy of Photodisc/Getty Images

* Imke Lass/Redux: p. viii

* Rosalie Winard: pp. ii–iii, 8, 10, 13, 58, 113, 122, 130

* Laurie Gardos: p. 36

* Cheryl Miller: pp. 124, 125, 126

* Jackie Rose: p. 52

* Academic Therapy Publications: p. 64

* Erika Voogd: pp. 118, 119

* Jeff Kravits/Getty Images: p. 141

INDEX

Page numbers in *italics* refer to photos and illustrations.